Jun 2017

Mexico is the birthplace of vanilla and chocolate, so it's no wonder that the country has a rich and revered ice cream tradition. Add tropical fruits, chiles, and nuts to the mix and you have the incomparable flavors of *Mexican Ice Cream*. Here, Mexico City native Fany Gerson explores everything from the country's established *heladerías* (ice cream parlors) to its colorful mobile carts and roadside stands, gathering together the best recipes for classics such as Oaxacan-style Lime Sorbet, Tres Leches Ice Cream, Chocolate-Chile Ice Cream, and Horchata Ice Cream with Cinnamon. With essays on Mexican ice cream culture and a guide to ingredients and equipment, *Mexican Ice Cream* will bring transporting, delicious ice cream to your home.

MEXICAN ICE CREAM

FANY GERSON

Photography by Justin Walker and
Fernando Gomez Carbajal

MEXICAN ICE CREAM

BELOVED RECIPES AND STORIES

TEN SPEED PRESS
California | New York

Para mi querido Cuttler con enorme agradecimiento
y cariño por el color, la dulzura y la inspiración
que creaste en mi vida y permanecerá latente.
Te quiero y te extraño.

CONTENTS

INTRODUCTION · 1

INTRODUCTION

"The best ice cream is the one you like the best."

—A SIGN AT LA ESPECIAL DE PARIS IN MEXICO CITY

Many years ago, I returned to my hometown of Mexico City while I waited for a working U.S. visa so I could start my first job as a pastry chef, at Rosa Mexicano restaurant in New York City. I wanted to research traditional Mexican desserts and sweets, and my Aunt Alex had heard from a friend about a town on the outskirts of Mexico City known for its amazing ice cream, worthy of a long drive. My aunt, sister, and I ventured out to the area of Xochimilco without an address; we were told that we'd find out where to go simply by asking around.

After several hours of driving, we finally found what we were looking for. It wasn't a town, but rather a highway lined on one side with about fifteen ice cream stands, each with colorful wooden barrels and vibrant handwritten signs displaying poetic and playful ice cream names, like "kiss of an angel," "Cinderella's dream," and "mermaid's song." Those barrels hid the most amazing ice creams I had ever tried. Between the three of us, we must have sampled close to twenty flavors. Our favorites included an ice cream infused with Maria cookies (vanilla tea biscuits) that was, to our surprise, smooth and free of chunks; tres leches made with sweetened cheese curds; *cajeta* (tangy goat's milk caramel); *guanabana* (soursop) sorbet studded with seeds and pulp; and my go-to flavor, tamarind sorbet sprinkled with chile.

Perhaps it was the surreal setting, the magic of all those handmade ice creams gathered together in one place, the adventure of seeking them out without really knowing where we were going, or the fact that I could taste the love and pride that went into making each and every one that we tried—whatever the reason, I knew right then that my life would never be the same.

Years later, while living in New York and working as a pastry chef, I found myself dreaming of those ice creams. I could still taste in my mind the *queso fresco* ice cream that struck the perfect balance of sweet and salty. I could visualize the man with a sweet smile using a long, well-worn wooden paddle to stir and scrape the ice cream as it froze, and I could hear the ice as it danced around in the metal cylinder. I made up my mind to bring handmade Mexican ice cream and frozen treats to the States so more people could discover the same delicious flavors that I tasted at those roadside stands.

Although ice cream was my true passion, I had difficulty keeping my business idea focused—I wanted not only an ice cream shop but a Mexican bakery, a candy shop, and a *churrería* (churro shop). Finally, in 2010, La Newyorkina was born. I was working two jobs at the time and was renting a bakery I could work at in the evenings, often around midnight. My friend Hannah and I started making *paletas* (ice pops) to sell at the Hester Street Fair. *Paletas* are quintessential frozen treats in Mexico, and they were the perfect way to test the concept and to gauge which traditional flavors most resonated with New Yorkers. I was pleasantly surprised by how popular they became. I made close to nine hundred *paletas* to sell at our first

weekend at the fair, and we sold out within a few hours. A year later, I started selling ice cream made in very small batches at the New Amsterdam Market when the market was located near the South Street Seaport. I purchased a lot of the produce and dairy from farmers there—ingredients that I used to make ice cream flavors such as *cajeta*, *horchata*, milk curd, Oaxacan chocolate, and avocado. People were very excited and wanted to find out where they could get more.

I had plans to open a brick-and-mortar store, but in 2012, my production kitchen was very badly affected by Hurricane Sandy and repairs took a long time, so the storefront was put on hold. In the summer of 2014, I turned a room with electrical meters in the front part of our production space into what we call La Tiendita, or "little store." La Tiendita isn't a retail store per se—during the week while we work, customers ring a doorbell and we attend to them. It has become something similar to a speakeasy for ice cream and *paletas*.

In 2015, I started making ice cream to order and to sell to restaurants, and in the fall of 2016 I opened my first true brick-and-mortar shop to introduce even more New Yorkers to the wonderful world of Mexican *helados* and *nieves*. So you can now come and try some of these treats for yourself! But don't worry if you can't make it to New York, or even Mexico, as this book will give you the information you need to make a variety of delicious flavors that will surely transport you.

A BRIEF HISTORY OF MEXICAN ICE CREAM

The history of ice cream in Mexico dates back to pre-Hispanic times. It is believed that the culture of the Teotihuacanos, in the center of Mexico, was the first to introduce this delicacy. People collected snow from the tops of volcanoes and are said to have buried it in pits that provided insulation. The main use for this snow was food preservation for the emperors, and it was highly valued because of the effort involved in obtaining it. After the Spaniards conquered Mexico in the sixteenth century, they sold the right to the collection and sale of snow, as well as to the production and sale of frozen treats, to the highest bidder, thereby establishing a monopoly. The high cost of snow collection and treat production meant that only members of the upper class could afford such luxuries.

In the nineteenth century, Mexico gained its independence, and the end of the monopoly over the collection and sale of snow meant that people from all levels of society could sample frozen treats. Some time later, Ice-production machin ery from Europe arrived, and the benefits that went along with this technology became available to the masses.

In the early twentieth century, many Italian immigrants found their way to Mexico, and they brought with them the tradition of gelato making. This is very likely why Mexican ice cream is similar to gelato in its texture and richness. In 1939, Pietro Chiandoni, who immigrated to Mexico from Italy at the age of fourteen and later became a famous boxer, opened his namesake ice cream shop in Mexico City. Even as ice cream became more popular, and the number of shops grew, Chiandoni remained one of the most popular shops in the city, as it still is today.

Ice cream making in Mexico, is primarily a lifelong craft that is handed down from generation to generation, and passing along the recipes and formulas is an oral tradition. During my research, I met several women in their seventies and eighties who still woke up at five or six o'clock in the morning to prepare the bases for the ice creams and sorbets to be sold that day. Churning the bases into sorbet or ice cream, a process known as *nevar*, is typically a man's job, and the *neveros* arrive once the bases are ready. But times are changing, and it is becoming more difficult for small family-run businesses to compete with big companies that mass-produce inexpensive ice cream. The rising cost of quality ingredients means lower profits, and younger generations are lured away by more lucrative pursuits. But I am an eternal optimist who believes that the dedication of craftspeople like those whom I met during my research, combined with Mexicans' simple love of good food, means that traditional Mexican ice cream will endure.

WHAT MAKES MEXICAN ICE CREAM SPECIAL?

Many places are known for their frozen treats. Italy has gelato, India has *kulfi*, and Turkey has *dondurma*. Mexico isn't particularly well-known for its ice cream, so you might be wondering what makes it so special that it deserves its very own cookbook. But there is so much that makes it unique and worth celebrating!

In Mexico, many makers of traditional ice cream still use *leche bronca*, unpasteurized raw milk, fresh from the farm, and milk from grass-fed cows is considered to yield the best-tasting ice cream. The milk is first boiled, and the skin, or *nata*, that forms on the surface may be removed (it makes a delicious spread for toast), though some makers prefer to leave the *nata* on the milk. The owner of Nevería la Pacanda in Pátzcuaro, Michoacán, one of my favorite *neverías*, says some producers who are more concerned about profits cut corners by using *leche bautizada*, or baptized milk, so called because the milk is diluted with water, but the quality is not as good.

The use of *garrafas* to churn the ice cream makes Mexican ice cream unique. A *garrafa* is a large metal cylinder that is placed inside a wooden barrel and surrounded by ice and coarse salt. The ice cream base is then poured into the *garrafa*, and a *nevero* stirs by hand using a long wooden or metal paddle and dancelike movements. As the base freezes on the sides of the *garrafa*, it is scraped off and moved to the center until the ice cream is thick and mostly

frozen. This hand-churning method incorporates a minimal amount of air into the ice cream, and this denser texture, along with a lower fat content, makes Mexican ice cream more similar to Italian gelato than to American-style ice cream. This traditional *garrafa* method is labor-intensive, and ice creams made this way usually have to be eaten the same day because they will become too hard if they are saved for the next. This is why some producers use commercial ice cream bases, so the product can be sold over a few days.

In Mexico, sorbets are just as popular as ice cream, and I think they're particularly good because even many commercial types are not made with artificial flavors, as good fruit is so abundant. One of the things I miss most about Mexico is the vast array of fresh fruits—ones that aren't available in New York and many that don't even have English names, such as *zapote negro*, *nanche*, *jobo*, and *marañón*. There isn't one single rule of how sorbets are made in Mexico, but for the most part they are made with lots of fruit, sugar, water, and sometimes guar gum. They are also made in *garrafas* and churned by hand.

The flavors of classic Mexican ice creams and sorbets are typically pure and simple—they highlight the main ingredient, whether it's orange, pecan, pink pine nut, *requesón* cheese, or cinnamon. But it's not uncommon to see flavor combinations with very colorful names, such as *seda de novia* (bride's silk), *beso de angel* (kiss of an angel), and *oración a los muertos* (prayer for the dead). Modern ice cream flavors tend to incorporate ingredients or elements from other aspects of Mexican cuisine—for example, *horchata* ice cream and *mole* ice cream. Nowadays, most shops and street vendors offer both classic and modern flavors, and American favorites like cookies and cream are creeping into the mix, too.

Sadly, handmade Mexican ice cream is a tradition that is slowly disappearing, so I feel it is important to appreciate and celebrate it to help keep it alive. Fortunately, there are still many passionate ice cream makers who are committed to continuing the tradition, and whose dedication and knowledge truly inspire me. It is their carefully and lovingly crafted *helados* and *nieves* that I pay homage to in the frozen treats I make at La Newyorkina, as well as in the pages of this book. Trust me when I say you do not need *leche bronca* or *garrafas* to make amazingly delicious Mexican-style ice cream at home. Just a trip to your local Latin American grocery store and a standard electric ice cream machine are all that's required to capture the vibrant flavors and exuberant spirit of authentic Mexican ice creams and sorbets. I hope the recipes in this book inspire you to discover a new world of tastes, textures, and frozen treats.

NiEVES LiGHT
·LECHE QUEMADA
TUNA
NIAGARA
LECHE QUEMADA
Beso de ANGEL
LIMON
SORBETE
NIAGARA Especial
TUNA
NUEZ
Beso OAXAQUEÑO
GUANABANA
COCO
ENCANTO OAXAQUEÑO·
MANGO c/ CHILE
CAJETA
ZARZAMORA
TAMARINDO c/ CHILE
FRESA
ARANDANO
CHAMOY c/ CHILE
ROSAS
TEQUILA
MARACUYA c/ CHILE
MAMEY
MEZCAL
NANCHE
QUESO
PIÑA COLADA
CHICOZAPOTE
ELOTE
CACAHUATE
DURAZNO
CHOCOLATE
CAPUCHINO
PISTACHE

Helado versus *Nieve*

Growing up in Mexico City, I always knew *helado* as ice cream and *nieve* as sorbet (as an adjective, *helado* means "frozen"; *nieve* also translates as "snow"). I'm pretty sure I kept referring to them that way until I started paying close attention to the terminology and not just how good these things tasted. Plus, no one ever told me otherwise.

But it turns out that in some Mexican states, both sorbet and ice cream are called *nieve*; *nieve de leche* or *nieve de crema* for ice cream, and *nieve de agua* for sorbet. In others, sorbet and ice cream made with milk are *nieve*, while ice cream made with cream is *helado*. In others still, *helado* is any frozen treat made in a machine. Some folks believe *helado* is ice cream made from a commercial base, while others say the opposite, that *helado* is handmade, high-quality ice cream.

It's all quite confusing—even for a native Spanish speaker—and since there isn't one hard-and-fast rule to follow, when I named the recipes in this book in Spanish, I chose to go with the term used by the source of inspiration for that particular recipe. And in some cases, history or tradition influenced the recipe name. So not all *nieves* are sorbets, and not all *helados* are made using the *garrafas* method. Each recipe has its own story to tell—and even better yet, to taste!

INGREDIENTS

It may sound obvious, but it's really important to buy the very best and freshest ingredients you can find. Use organic dairy and eggs if you can, fruits that are at the height of their season, top-quality chocolate, and the most fragrant spices you can get your hands on.

You will be familiar with many of the ingredients used in this book—for example, milk, sugar, and salt—but I thought it would be helpful to offer some guidance about ones that might be new to you and those that are essential for making the most delicious frozen treats. Nowadays, there are many sources for international ingredients, including Latin American grocers, well-stocked supermarkets, specialty stores, and online merchants.

I encourage you to be adventurous and explore. Discovering new ingredients and exciting flavors is part of the fun!

Avocados
In Mexico, there are many, many varieties of avocados, including one with a thin, smooth edible skin that my mom absolutely loves. Of the much more limited options in the United States, I prefer Hass avocados. This variety is harvested while underripe and changes from dark green to black with a purplish hue as it ripens. To judge whether an avocado is ripe, gently squeeze it—if it yields a bit, it's ready

to use. If you feel a gap between the skin and the flesh, discard the avocado.

Cinnamon
Canela is Spanish for "cinnamon." Mexican cinnamon is more flavorful and fragrant than the more common cassia variety, often referred to as "regular" cinnamon. Mexican cinnamon is also called "true" or Ceylon cinnamon. Look for large pieces that are sold in bulk so you can break one apart and smell the sweet fragrance that will undoubtedly make you smile. If you need ground *canela*, I highly recommend that you use an electric coffee grinder to grind pieces into a powder—the flavor will be much more intense because the oils are fresh. If you can't find whole Mexican cinnamon, it's fine to purchase ground Ceylon cinnamon. Cassia would work but the flavor is different, more spicy as opposed to fruity, so I would avoid using it in these recipes.

Chamoy

The origins of the sauce known as *chamoy* are uncertain, but it is believed to have been derived from Japanese *umeboshi*, or salted preserved plums. To make *chamoy*, plums or apricots are pickled in brine, and vinegar is often added. The pickled fruits are eaten with a bit of the liquid, or the liquid is eaten on its own. *Chamoy*, red in color and sold in bottles, is often used as a topping on fruit-based frozen treats; look for it in Latin American markets.

Chiles

In Mexico, the variety of chiles, both fresh and dried, is vast. Recipes in this book use a few types of fresh chiles and a handful of different dried ones. Try to purchase your chiles from a Mexican market or specialty purveyor so you can be sure that you're getting the right variety and that they are fragrant and flavorful.

Jalapeños, serranos, and habaneros are the fresh chiles used in this book. Jalapeños are 2 to 3 inches long, dark green in color, and mildly spicy. Serranos look similar to jalapeños but are more slender, and their flavor is a bit sweeter and spicier. If you can't find serranos, you can use jalapeños instead. Habaneros are bell shaped, orange in color, and intensely spicy. Be very careful when handling them.

Piquín chiles, tiny dried red chiles with spicy, citrusy notes, are commonly used in Mexico for mixing into or sprinkling on *nieves*. Slightly larger and longer and very spicy árbol chiles are often used to flavor and garnish *nieves*. Piquín and árbol chiles are sold both whole and ground; the recipe will specify the type to use. In some cases, cayenne can be used in place of ground piquín or árbol chile; again, the recipe will let you know.

Guar Gum

Guar gum is a flour-like substance made from the guar bean. It is used as a thickener and emulsifier in both ice cream making and baking. It has become more widely available in recent years as it's often used in gluten-free baked goods.

Hibiscus

Hibiscus flowers, called *flores de Jamaica*, are sold dried in Mexican grocery stores and many natural food stores. With a sour, acidic flavor, they are used mainly for infusions and release a beautiful fuchsia hue when soaked in liquid.

Limes

Mexicans love limes! The Spanish word for lime is *limón*, which sometimes causes confusion because *limón* sounds closer to "lemon" than to "lime." (To make it even more confusing, there is another citrus fruit, called *lima*, that grows in the Yucatán region; to me, it has a flavor somewhere between a lemon and a lime, with perfume notes.) To choose the juiciest limes, squeeze them gently—they should give a little to the pressure.

Mangoes

There are several varieties of mangoes in Mexico, but the three varieties that are widely available in the United States are *manila*, a small, yellow mango with a juicy, creamy, sweet flesh; *ataulfo*, which is similar to the manila and the champagne mango but is more fibrous and stringy; and *criollo* or *petacón*, a large, meaty mango that is widely exported. Whichever type you choose to use, if the fruits are hard, let them ripen at room temperature until they yield to gentle pressure and are fragrant. Frozen mango can be substituted if you have difficulty finding good fresh mango; thaw it in the refrigerator overnight before using.

Mexican Chocolate

Mexican chocolate, used for making hot chocolate, is often sold in disks or tablets. Commonly flavored with Mexican cinnamon and sometimes made with almonds or peanuts, it has a granular texture. Commercial brands such as Ibarra and Abuelita are available in many supermarkets, but I always seek out varieties made from cacao that has been toasted over coal or wood and ground by hand because of its wonderfully complex flavor characteristics. Brands I like include Seasons of My Heart from Oaxaca, and Taza, which is a bit more tannic than others; Rancho Gordo also offers Mexican chocolate that is quite good. Oaxaca is known for producing amazing chocolate, though the cacao is grown in the states of Chiapas and Tabasco.

Mexican Vanilla

Vanilla is native to Papantla, Veracruz, and to this day, this location is the source of most Mexican vanilla. Mexican vanilla has a sweet, creamy, caramel-like flavor with hint of spice. If you're buying pods, choose ones that are plump; if you're purchasing extract, seek out good-quality pure extract. Mexican vanilla may be difficult to source due to availability; if you have trouble finding some, use vanilla from Madagascar or Tahiti.

Nopales

These paddles from the prickly pear cactus are available year-round. Look for ones that are bright green and a bit soft but not limp. If it's your first time working with them, you may want to wear rubber gloves to protect your hands from the many thorns. Rinse the *nopales* under cold water. Then, using a small sharp knife, scrape off each bump where a thorn was attached, being careful not to remove too much flesh. Rinse again and check to make sure that you have removed all bumps and thorns. You should also trim the edges, as they sometimes have hard bits or tiny thorns you can't really see. The flavor is very "green" and acidic.

Piloncillo

A type of unrefined cane sugar also known as *panela* and *panocha*, *piloncillo* can vary in color from dark blond to brown. It is commonly shaped into cones, though in some Mexican markets you can find rounds and even ground *piloncillo*. The cones can be difficult to cut, but I find that using a serrated or chef's knife and cutting little by little at an angle is an effective technique. If you can't find *piloncillo*, dark brown sugar is a good substitute, as both have a molasses-like flavor.

Queso Fresco

Queso fresco, which translates as "fresh cheese," is a crumbly cow's milk cheese that is slightly salty and mildly acidic. In a pinch, you can substitute farmer cheese but also add a bit of salt, as farmer cheese is less salty than *queso fresco*.

Requesón

Requesón is a slightly grainy, mildly salty cow's milk cheese with texture somewhere between ricotta and cottage cheese. Look for it in Latin American grocery stores. If you can't find *requesón*, ricotta cheese with enough salt mixed in to give it a slight saltiness is a good substitute.

Tamarind

Tamarind grows as dark brown pods around a sticky, seed-studded flesh; the hard outer shell must be removed before use. It is sold in several forms: whole pods, blocks of pulp, puree, and seedless concentrate. Purchase whole pods or pulp, as indicated in the recipe you're making. Both are commonly available in Latin American markets and Asian grocery stores. Tamarind has a sweet-tart flavor, but Mexican tamarind is more sour and acidic than the Asian variety.

EQUIPMENT

When it comes to tools for making ice cream, you could get geeky and equip your kitchen with high-tech thermometers and appliances, but there's really no need to. In Mexico, some of the best ice creams and sorbets are made by street vendors who prepare everything by hand. Still, some basic pieces of kitchen equipment will make the process much more enjoyable.

Blender

Many recipes in this book require pureeing, and a blender is the best tool for the job. A sturdy standing model works quickly and effectively, but for most recipes, you can use a handheld blender instead—you'll simply need to take more time to move the blender around in the mixture and ensure it's well processed.

Digital Kitchen Scale

Although I prefer to use weight instead of volume measurements for greater accuracy, the recipes in this book call mostly for volume measurements of ingredients. However, there are some ingredients that are best weighed, so I recommend purchasing an inexpensive digital kitchen scale. You may find that you, too, prefer weighing your ingredients.

Food Processor

A food processor is great for chopping nuts, grinding sugar with citrus zest, and pureeing thick mixtures like chile paste. It can also be used for pureeing liquids, but be aware of your food processor's maximum capacity for liquids; if overfilled the bowl may leak.

Ice Cream Machine

All of the recipes in this book that use an ice cream machine were tested in an electric machine made for home use, and some were even churned by hand in an ice-chilled cylinder, mimicking the *garrafa* technique from Mexico.

A basic electric ice cream machine works well and won't break the bank. You do have to remember to put the canister in the freezer a day in advance, and unless you have multiple canisters, you won't be able to spin more than one batch a day because the canister has to be completely frozen before each use. Keep in mind that the canister will occupy a fair amount of space in the freezer.

If you are planning to make lots and lots of ice cream (and I encourage you to do so), I suggest you invest in a machine with a built-in cooling unit so that you can whip up batches at a moment's notice. But keep in mind that these appliances are heavy and will occupy a lot of space on your kitchen counter. They are also expensive, although you can sometimes find used ones online or in thrift stores.

Not to be overlooked, an old-fashioned hand-crank ice cream machine that requires ice and rock salt is always fun. The result might not be as creamy as one made in an electric machine, but in fact, it will be more similar in texture to traditional Mexican ice cream made in a *garrafa*.

Measuring Cups and Spoons

It may sound obvious, but for accuracy, use a liquid measuring cup to measure liquids and dry measuring cups to measure dry ingredients. When measuring a dry ingredient, mound it into the measuring cup or measuring spoon and then level the top with a straight edge (like the blade of an icing spatula).

Microplane Grater

A Microplane grater is my favorite tool for finely grating just about anything. It's particularly good for zesting citrus, as it shaves off just a thin layer and allows you to control how much of the peel you remove.

Saucepans

Choose heavy saucepans, as they distribute heat more evenly. This is particularly important when cooking custard ice cream bases and when caramelizing sugar, as for *cajeta* and passion fruit caramel. If the mixture you're cooking is at all acidic, make sure the saucepan is nonreactive, otherwise the food may wind up with a metallic flavor and an off color.

Silicone Spatula

Some mixtures need to be stirred while cooking, and a silicone spatula is the best tool for the job. The wide, flexible, heatproof blade is better than the stiff, rounded bowl of a wooden spoon for scraping along the bottom and sides of a pan to prevent burning and sticking.

Spice Grinder

A spice grinder is great for turning bits of *canela* into powder and for making small amounts of ground chile from dried whole chiles. A manual spice grinder works nicely, but so does an electric coffee grinder—just make sure that the coffee grinder is dedicated to spices so that the flavors aren't transferred to your coffee (and vice versa).

Strainer

A fine-mesh strainer is the best tool for straining lumps out of custard ice cream bases and for removing seeds and bits of skin from fruit purees. When straining purees, pressing firmly on the solids in the strainer extracts as much liquid as possible, so it helps to use a sturdy, well-made strainer that can hold up to the pressure.

Whisks

Look for whisks with stainless steel wires. There are several different types, but the most common ones are sauce whisks (also called French whisks and straight whisks) and balloon whisks. A sauce whisk has a long, narrow shape and relatively stiff wires, making it sturdy enough for combining heavy batters and sauces. A balloon whisk has a large, bulbous head and delicate wires that are good for aerating egg whites, cream, and light batters. For most of the recipes in this book that require a whisk, a sauce whisk will work best.

Regional Ice Cream Specialties

Mexico offers many regional specialties, even within the category of frozen treats. Here are a few worth seeking out if you visit.

In Jerez, Zacatecas, *raspanieve* is shaved ice topped with fruit syrup, like guava or banana, a scoop or two of ice cream, and caramel.

In Jalisco, you will find street vendors with lovely ice creams that are in pencil-shaped metal molds. Each one is unmolded to order; many are striped with guava paste and resemble a candy cane.

In a town called Yecapixtla, each serving of ice cream is decorated with bright, colorful wafers in a variety of shapes, such as rabbits and birds.

In Yucatán, Dulcería y Sorbetería Colón, a personal favorite of mine, is a lovely ice cream shop that has been around for over a century. It's famous for *champola*, ice cream served in a tall glass with cold milk, like a milk shake minus the shaken part.

In the town of Dolores Hidalgo, a shop called La Flor de Dolores specializes in ice creams and sorbets made with cacti. In addition to cactus paddles (*nopales*) and prickly pears, which are quite common, they use other cacti fruits such as *garambullos*, *pitayas*, *xoconostle*, and *guamichi*. I can say with certainty that their *guamichi* sorbet is the very best flavor I've had in my life!

Michoacán is home to several specialties. In Pátzcuaro, *nieve de pasta* (page 56), or caramelized milk ice cream, reigns. Uruapan grows lots of macadamia nuts, so there macadamia ice cream is the star. In Zamora, *helado de chongos* (page 63), or milk curd ice cream, is a favorite.

In Oaxaca, *nieve de leche quemada*, or burnt milk ice cream (page 80), is the one to get. Traditionally, it's paired with *nieve de tuna roja*, or red prickly pear sorbet.

SORBETS

NIEVES DE AGUA

et me tell you, if it were up to me, I would write a book solely about sorbets. It's not that I don't love ice cream, but rather because I feel that sorbets are incredibly underrated. And yet they can be spectacular in both flavor and texture! There is nothing in the world more refreshing on a hot summer's day.

The quality of fruit in Mexico is amazing and the variety enormous; the array of sorbet flavors reflects this. I suppose it's why I'm always surprised at the small selection of sorbets in other countries I visit. Typically, raspberry and lemon are standard, with mango being the most exotic flavor on offer. Often, sorbet feels like an afterthought, created for those who don't eat ice cream.

In Mexico, however, enter an ice cream shop or visit a stand and you'll be overwhelmed by the variety of *nieves de agua* (sorbets). Scooped out of colorful metal containers (for the most part), the sorbets present an enticing rainbow of lovely hues. Fruits in their pure form are embraced—sorbets such as watermelon, guava, and prickly pear are often flecked with seeds, and some, such as *guanabana* (soursop), tamarind, and mango, even contain morsels of pulp that add texture and a burst of intense flavor. I definitely appreciate the rustic Mexican approach to sorbet making, as you'll see throughout this chapter.

While ice cream quality can vary greatly from shop to shop, *nieves de agua* tend to be of high quality across all of Mexico. This is in large part due to the fact that even high-volume commercial producers use real fruit. That's not to say extracts or other flavor enhancers aren't used (they definitely are), but most Mexican ice cream makers appreciate and understand the value of fresh fruit and use the very best they can afford. Some makers purchase huge quantities of fruits when they are in season, prepare them, and keep them frozen so that they're available for use

In Mexico, chile is a common flavoring for all types of sorbets. It might be ground chiles (mixed with salt) or chile sauce; the chile might be mixed directly into the sorbet, sprinkled into the serving cup before the sorbet is scooped in, or added on top like a garnish—or all of the above. *Chamoy* (pickled plum sauce, see page 12) is also a favorite addition for the salty, tangy flavor it brings. Some shops add a squeeze of fresh lime juice to servings of sorbet as well.

Some of the recipes in this chapter, such as Guava Sorbet (page 33) and Soursop Sorbet (page 46), are classic Mexican flavors, while others, like Pineapple-Herb Sorbet (page 30) and Avocado–Passion Fruit Sorbet (page 42), are more modern because they feature a blend of flavors. And don't pass up ones like Lime Sorbet (page 29) just because they sound basic—even super-simple flavors are delicious because of their brightness and pure fruit flavor. Just remember: when making sorbet, it's all about the fruit. Look for fragrant peaches, plump berries, and juicy oranges that are full of flavor and natural sugars. Sorbets made with amazing fruit will capture the essence and spirit of Mexico's wonderful *nieves de agua*.

year-round. (In Oaxaca, this is true of the prickly pear used to make *nieve de tuna roja*—not offering that flavor is comparable to not having vanilla on the menu at an American ice cream shop.) Others simply use whatever fresh fruits are in season, which makes each flavor special in its own way. Some fruits are unique to certain regions of Mexico, so you might find a flavor of sorbet sold in only one area—for example, *garambullo*, a cactus fruit that resembles blueberries, is available only in central Mexico, while *arrayán*, a small, tangy fruit with lots of seeds, is found in the state of Jalisco.

Smooth Sorbet

A well-made sorbet is creamy and smooth (not taking into consideration fruit chunks or bits added for texture). Achieving the perfect consistency is all about getting the right balance of ingredients.

Sugar adds sweetness, of course, but because it doesn't freeze, it also affects a sorbet's consistency. Granulated sugar requires liquid of some sort to dissolve the crystals, but if too much liquid is added, the sorbet will be icy and hard when frozen, and the flavor may be compromised. In this case, using some sugar in liquid rather than granulated form, such as honey or light corn syrup, can help keep the sorbet smooth. Just a tablespoon or two inhibits the formation of ice crystals during freezing, and the thickness of honey or corn syrup gives the sorbet base a little more body, which means a creamier consistency.

It's well-known that alcohol doesn't freeze. Adding just 2 to 3 tablespoons of alcohol per quart (of frozen sorbet) can have a big impact on the sorbet's consistency.

In Mexico, to ensure a good consistency, some sorbet makers add *cremola*, or guar gum, to their bases. This widely used emulsifier is a natural powder, and just a little bit does the trick. In the United States, guar gum can be found at many natural food stores and online.

Fruits that contain high amounts of pectin, a natural thickener, yield creamy sorbets without the help of corn syrup, alcohol, or guar gum. Peaches, raspberries, and mangoes are examples of pectin-rich fruits.

OAXACAN LIME SORBET

NIEVE DE LIMÓN OAXAQUEÑO

This lime sorbet is popular all over Oaxaca. Unlike Nieve de Limón (page 29), this one is made with only lime zest and no juice, so the flavor is very intense but without any tartness. The bright green color may appear artificial but is the result of using so much grated lime zest.

In Oaxaca, sorbet makers often use *tiernos* limes, which are immature limes that have a very strong flavor but do not yield much juice. I find that Key limes are similar in taste to *tiernos*, but you can use any kind, really. Try to find small, dark-colored limes for the best flavor, and be sure to wash and dry them carefully before zesting.

MAKES ABOUT
· 1 ·
QUART

12 Key limes, washed and dried

1 cup sugar

3¾ cups water

1 tablespoon light corn syrup

Pinch of kosher salt

Grate the zest from the limes, removing as much of the green skin as possible and avoiding the white pith. In a blender or food processor, combine the zest and sugar and pulse 4 or 5 times to extract the natural oils. Transfer the sugar mixture to a bowl, add the water, corn syrup, and salt, and whisk until the sugar dissolves. Cover and refrigerate until cold, at least 2 hours but no more than 4 hours.

Freeze and churn in an ice cream maker according to the manufacturer's instructions. For a soft consistency, serve the sorbet right away; for a firmer consistency, transfer it to a container, cover, and allow to harden in the freezer for 2 to 3 hours.

SORBETS

LIME SORBET

NIEVE DE LIMÓN

One of the most popular ice cream shops in Mexico City is a lovely family-run business called Nevería Roxy. The multiple locations are recognizable for their '50s décor and known for using artisan methods. The founder, Carlos Gallardo, has been making *nieves* since 1945. I visited the shop on the now very trendy Colonia Condesa and chatted for a couple of hours with Mr. Gallardo's wife and one of his daughters. Of the many stories they shared, my favorite was about the lime sorbet that made Mr. Gallardo famous: customers criticized its color—or lack thereof. They couldn't believe that the white-colored sorbet was lime flavor! Indeed, many lime ice creams and sorbets in Mexico are made with green food coloring and to this day, some people are turned off by the absence of color. But anyone who tastes this citrusy, sweet-and-tangy treat would agree that food coloring couldn't possibly make it any more delicious or refreshing.

MAKES ABOUT
· 1¼ ·
QUARTS

1¾ cups water
2 cups sugar
2 cups freshly squeezed lime juice
1 teaspoon guar gum (see page 13)

In a small saucepan, combine the water and sugar and cook over medium heat, stirring, until the sugar dissolves, about 1 minute. Pour the mixture into a bowl and allow to cool for 10 minutes. Stir in the lime juice. Add the guar gum and whisk until it dissolves. Cover the bowl and refrigerate until cold, at least 2 hours or up to overnight.

Freeze and churn in an ice cream maker according to the manufacturer's instructions. For a soft consistency, serve the sorbet right away; for a firmer consistency, transfer it to a container, cover, and allow to harden in the freezer for 2 to 3 hours.

PINEAPPLE-HERB SORBET

NIEVE DE PIÑA-HIERBA

Guadalajara, the second-largest city in Mexico, is well-known for its *nieves*, and Nevería San Antonio is one of my favorite shops. Famous for its small counter with rows and rows of *garrafas*, barrels used for hand-churning ice cream, the shop has modernized and expanded since I was a child, but the ice cream is still as good as I remember.

On my last visit to Guadalajara, I drove straight from the airport to the *nevería* to try one of their seasonal flavors, *nieve de piña-hierba*, or pineapple-herb sorbet. It was so good I had to go the next day to get more. The flavor of pineapple is very refreshing, and it pairs beautifully with any kind of herb. Nevería San Antonio used spearmint for their version, but try it with lemon thyme or basil for something different. Have fun and make it your own!

MAKES ABOUT
· 1 ·
QUART

1 small pineapple, cored, peeled, and cut into chunks (about 3 cups)

1 cup sugar

1 cup water

Juice of 1 lime

1 teaspoon kosher salt

2 tablespoons chopped fresh herb, such as mint, basil, or rosemary

In a blender or food processor, puree the pineapple chunks, sugar, water, lime juice, and salt until smooth. Add the herb and pulse until the herb is broken down into green specks. Pour the mixture into a bowl, cover, and refrigerate the base until cold, at least 3 hours or up to overnight.

Whisk the base gently to recombine. Freeze and churn in an ice cream maker according to the manufacturer's instructions. For a soft consistency, serve the sorbet right away; for a firmer consistency, transfer it to a container, cover, and allow to harden in the freezer for 2 to 3 hours.

PEACH SORBET

NIEVE DE DURAZNO

Nieves Chagüita is perhaps the most well-known *nevería* in Oaxaca. Located in the Benito Juárez Market, the stand is bright and colorful and the *nieves* are made daily on the premises. Run by the marvelous Dinorah Allende, one of the sweetest and kindest women I've ever met, the shop has been around for five generations. Dinorah believes that La Chagüita stands out from the competition not so much because of its *nieves* but because she treats all of her customers like family. She says she is in the business of making people happy. While La Chagüita offers many popular flavors, this peach sorbet is the one I always get if the fruits are in season.

Peaches in Mexico tend to be a little firmer and more tart than ones found in cooler climates. If yours are super sweet, reduce the sugar to ¾ cup. You could use any type of peach (yellow or white) in this recipe, and even nectarines, too.

MAKES ABOUT
▪ 1 ▪
QUART

2½ pounds ripe peaches, washed and dried

2 teaspoons freshly squeezed lime juice

1 cup water

1 cup sugar

½ teaspoon kosher salt

Leaving the skins on the peaches, pit and dice the fruit. In a food processor or blender, working in batches if needed, combine the diced peaches, lime juice, water, sugar, and salt and puree until smooth and the sugar has dissolved, about 3 minutes. Pour the mixture into a bowl (if you prefer a smooth sorbet, pour the mixture through a fine-mesh strainer set over a bowl). Cover and refrigerate until cold, at least 2 hours or up to overnight.

Freeze and churn in an ice cream maker according to the manufacturer's instructions. For a soft consistency, serve the sorbet right away; for a firmer consistency, transfer it to a container, cover, and allow to harden in the freezer for 2 to 3 hours.

GUAVA SORBET

NIEVE DE GUAYABA

MAKES ABOUT
· 1 ·
QUART

As winter approaches in Mexico, markets start to smell of the sweet and very distinctive aroma of guavas. The skin of this small oval fruit is yellow or green, or somewhere in between, and can have pink or orange hues; the flesh is white, yellow, or bright pink and contains lots of seeds. The pink-fleshed variety is the one most commonly used for sorbets in Mexico; it has a wonderful perfume and a nice earthy quality, a bit like a pear. Traditionally, guava sorbet includes the seeds, but you can strain them out if you prefer; the yield will be significantly less.

2¼ pounds ripe
pink-fleshed guavas

1⅓ cups sugar

Juice of 1 lime

¼ teaspoon kosher salt

Trim off the ends of the guavas and cut each one lengthwise into quarters. In a saucepan, combine the guavas and sugar and set the pan over medium heat. Cook, stirring occasionally, until the guavas start to release their juice and are falling apart, about 30 minutes. Remove from the heat and allow to cool for about 10 minutes.

You can leave the guava mixture as is, or for a smoother sorbet, pass it through a fine-mesh strainer set over a bowl, pushing the fruit through the strainer with the back of a spoon or ladle. Discard the seeds and skin in the strainer. Stir in the lime juice and salt. Cover and refrigerate until cold, at least 3 hours or up to overnight.

Freeze and churn in an ice cream maker according to the manufacturer's instructions. For a soft consistency, serve the sorbet right away; for a firmer consistency, transfer it to a container, cover, and allow to harden in the freezer for 2 to 3 hours.

NOTE Make sure that the guavas you use are ripe—they should be soft and have an intense fragrance. If you can't find fresh ripe guavas, some grocery and specialty stores sell them frozen, so check the freezer aisle.

MANDARIN ORANGE SORBET

In November and December, different varieties of citrus begin to appear all around Mexico. One very special fruit is *mandarina reina*, or queen mandarin, likely named for its large size and incredible sweetness. It's delicious eaten out of hand, but Mexican sorbet makers prefer to use it and other juicier and slightly more acidic varieties to give their *nieve de mandarina* a nice balance of sweet and tart, as well as an intense flavor and fragrance.

You can use tangerines, clementines, or even oranges for this sorbet. Taste the juice after squeezing the fruits—if it is super sweet, use about 2 tablespoons less sugar.

MAKES ABOUT
· 1¼ ·
QUARTS

3½ cups freshly squeezed mandarin orange juice

²/₃ cup sugar

2 tablespoons light corn syrup or honey

Pinch of kosher salt

In a small saucepan, combine about half of the mandarin orange juice with the sugar, corn syrup, and salt. Cook over low heat, stirring, until the sugar dissolves. Pour the mixture into a bowl and stir in the remaining juice. Cover and refrigerate until cold, at least 2 hours or up to overnight.

Freeze and churn in an ice cream maker according to the manufacturer's instructions. For a soft consistency, serve the sorbet right away; for a firmer consistency, transfer it to a container, cover, and allow to harden in the freezer for 2 to 3 hours.

NOTE To make a version of this sorbet with a kick, mix in ¼ cup of tequila just before putting the base in the refrigerator to chill. The alcohol will make the sorbet slightly softer as well.

CACTUS PADDLE SORBET WITH PINEAPPLE AND LIME

NIEVE DE NOPAL CON PIÑA Y LIMÓN

Cactus paddles, called *nopales*, are found all over Mexico, and I absolutely love them. They have a lightly acidic taste and a slightly slimy quality similar to that of okra, but you shouldn't be put off by it. The larger ones have a more pronounced sliminess, so if you find that texture unappealing, look for smaller *nopales*. Either way, use caution when cleaning them because they do have thorns.

The combination of *nopales*, pineapple, and lime is very popular for juice, and trust me—it makes an amazing *nieve*. When shopping, look for firm, deep green cactus paddles and pineapple that is very ripe.

MAKES ABOUT
· 1½ ·
QUARTS

¾ pound cactus paddles (nopales), cleaned (see page 15)

1½ cups coarse sea salt

¼ cup freshly squeezed lime juice

1½ cups diced pineapple (about ½ pineapple)

1 cup sugar

¾ cup water

2 tablespoons honey

Cut the cleaned cactus paddles into rough 1-inch squares. In a bowl, toss the cactus with the salt. Set aside at room temperature for 1 hour; the salt will extract the natural slime from the cactus.

Transfer the cactus to a colander and rinse under cold running water to remove all the salt and slime. Drain well. In a blender, puree the cactus, lime juice, pineapple, sugar, water, and honey until smooth. Pour the mixture into a bowl, cover, and refrigerate until cold, at least 2 hours or up to 5 hours.

Freeze and churn in an ice cream maker according to the manufacturer's instructions. For a soft consistency, serve the sorbet right away; for a firmer consistency, transfer it to a container, cover, and allow to harden in the freezer for 2 to 3 hours.

MEXICAN ICE CREAM

QUINCE SORBET

NIEVE DE MEMBRILLO

I included a recipe for *nieve de membrillo* in *My Sweet Mexico*, but I think quince sorbet is so special that I had to have a recipe in this book as well. I like the surprise of quince, as its dull color is in stark contrast to its explosive flavor. The recipe was given to me by Mrs. Lolita, the owner of Nevería Erendira in Pátzcuaro, Michoacán. Her father started the business in the 1930s and now the third generation is getting involved.

Quince is in season in the late fall and winter. Be sure to choose fruits with a sweet, floral fragrance, as these will be the ripest ones. The combination of quince and cinnamon simmering on the stove will fill the kitchen with a wonderful perfume that will surely make you smile.

MAKES ABOUT
· 1 ·
QUART

1½ pounds ripe quinces (about 4 small to medium)

6 cups water

1 (3-inch) piece Mexican cinnamon

¾ cup sugar

Juice of ½ lemon

Pinch of kosher salt

Peel, quarter, and core the quinces. Put the pieces in a saucepan and add the water, cinnamon, and sugar. Cook, uncovered, over medium heat, stirring occasionally, until the quince is very tender, about 30 minutes, making sure the mixture is always at a simmer and never boils. Remove from the heat, cover, and let cool for 2 to 3 hours; the color will darken during this time.

Remove and discard the cinnamon. Transfer the quince mixture to a blender, add the lemon juice and salt, and puree until smooth. Pour the mixture through a fine-mesh strainer set over a bowl. Cover and refrigerate until cold, at least 2 hours or up to overnight.

Freeze and churn in an ice cream maker according to the manufacturer's instructions. For a soft consistency, serve the sorbet right away; for a firmer consistency, transfer it to a container, cover, and allow to harden in the freezer for 2 to 3 hours.

CORN AND CACAO SORBET

NIEVE DE POZOL

Pozol, a traditional cold, frothy beverage made of corn and cacao and served in round gourds called *jicaras*, can be traced back to pre-Colombian Mexico. Initially called *pochotl*, which roughly translates as "sparkling," it is still enjoyed widely and is often made in different flavors. My favorite combination, with cinnamon, is the inspiration for this recipe.

Although I like to make this sorbet with heirloom corn from Mexico and fresh cacao beans, this recipe calls for easier-to-find masa harina (ground corn flour dough) and a combination of Dutch-process cocoa and unsweetened chocolate. The mouthfeel is slightly grainy but wonderfully rich for a sorbet.

MAKES ABOUT
· 1½ ·
QUARTS

½ cup masa harina

2½ cups water, plus more as needed

1 cup sugar

½ cup unsweetened Dutch-process cocoa powder

Pinch of kosher salt

¾ teaspoon ground Mexican cinnamon

5 ounces bittersweet or semisweet chocolate, finely chopped

In a bowl, combine the masa harina with ½ cup of the water. Mix with your hands until you have a uniform dough. If it feels a bit dry, mix in a couple more tablespoons of water and set aside.

In a large saucepan, whisk together the remaining 2 cups of water and the sugar, cocoa powder, and salt. Bring to a boil over medium heat, whisking continuously to melt the sugar. Add the masa mixture, return to a boil, and cook, whisking continuously, until the mixture is well combined and there are absolutely no lumps, about 3 minutes. Whisk in the cinnamon and chocolate, until the chocolate is melted. Transfer the base to a bowl, cover, and refrigerate until cold, about 2 hours.

Whisk the base to recombine. Freeze and churn in an ice cream maker according to the manufacturer's instructions. For a soft consistency, serve the sorbet right away; for a firmer consistency, transfer it to a container, cover, and freeze for no more than 1 hour before serving.

NOTE If you can find fresh masa, use 8 ounces instead of the masa harina mixed with water. Fresh masa is often sold in Latin grocery stores and bodegas.

SORBETS

39

MIXED BERRIES SORBET

NIEVE DE FRUTOS ROJOS

Frutos rojos means "red fruits." Such a generic name allows for any type of berries to be used in the *nieve*, depending on what is available and in season. The state of Michoacán, for example, has some of the best blackberries I've ever tasted. They are small and a bit acidic, so a sorbet made with them is slightly tart. In Guanajuato, *nieve de frutos rojos* is often made with sweet, bright red strawberries that have a floral flavor and aroma. My suggestion is to simply make this recipe your own by using whatever type of berries you like, as long as they're fresh and flavorful.

Macerating the berries before pureeing releases their natural juices, and the little bit of lime juice brightens their flavors. Leaving the seeds in the puree gives the sorbet a lovely texture.

MAKES ABOUT
· 1 ·
QUART

3 cups mixed berries, such as raspberries, blackberries, blueberries, and sliced strawberries

1 cup sugar

2 cups water

Juice of 1 lime

½ teaspoon kosher salt

In a bowl, toss together all of the berries and the sugar. Allow the berries to macerate at room temperature for 1 hour, until they release their juice.

Transfer the berries and their juice to a blender or food processor and add the water, lime juice, and salt. Pulse until well combined. Transfer to a container, cover, and refrigerate until cold, at least 2 hours or up to overnight.

Freeze and churn in an ice cream maker according to the manufacturer's instructions. For a soft consistency, serve the sorbet right away; for a firmer consistency, transfer it to a container, cover, and allow to harden in the freezer for 2 to 3 hours.

SORBETS

AVOCADO-PASSION FRUIT SORBET

NIEVE DE AGUACATE CON MARACUYÁ

MAKES ABOUT
· 1 ·
QUART

2 cups fresh or thawed frozen passion fruit puree

¾ cup plus 2 tablespoons sugar

2 small ripe avocados

½ teaspoon kosher salt

1 tablespoon freshly squeezed lime juice

The state of Michoacán grows amazing avocados—many are exported to the United States—so it's no surprise that it's where I found inspiration for this recipe. This particular combination of avocado and passion fruit was one I tried in the form of a *paleta* (a Mexican ice pop) in Morelia, the capitol of Michoacán. The acidity of passion fruit cuts through the richness of avocado, while still complementing its flavor in a very unexpected way. Avocados are so luscious and velvety that you can make a perfectly creamy sorbet, like this one, without adding any emulsifiers.

In a small saucepan, combine the passion fruit puree and sugar. Cook over medium-high heat, stirring, until the sugar dissolves. Remove from the heat and allow to cool to room temperature.

Cut the avocados in half lengthwise. Remove the pits and scoop the flesh into a blender or food processor. Add the cooled passion fruit mixture and the salt and process until smooth, scraping down the sides of the blender jar or bowl as needed. Add the lime juice and process just until combined. Pour the mixture into a bowl, cover, and refrigerate until cold, about 2 hours.

Freeze and churn in an ice cream maker according to the manufacturer's instructions. For a soft consistency, serve the sorbet right away; for a firmer consistency, transfer it to a container, cover, and allow to harden in the freezer for 2 to 3 hours.

NOTE Look for frozen passion fruit puree in Latin American markets and specialty grocery stores.

STRAWBERRY, PINEAPPLE, AND ORANGE SORBET

NIEVE DE OASIS (FRESA, PIÑA Y NARANJA)

I traveled to Puebla in central Mexico as part of Chefs on a Plane, a trip for New York–based chefs and mixologists organized by Puebla's Ministry of Tourism. My dear friend Gus—one of the funniest people I know—was also on that trip. During our free time, he accompanied me as I did research for this book. One of the places we visited was El Carmen—or the "true" El Carmen, as locals know it—although the sign displayed says Super Paletería Mary Barragán. (There is another *nevería* called El Carmen a few blocks away, opened by a brother of the owner of the original shop after a falling-out.) We tried about twenty flavors during that visit and decided this was the one to beat.

In Mexico, *oasis* is a popular name for juices and sorbets that have three or four different fruits, and this is one of the most common combinations. The sweetness from the berries and the slight acidity from the orange and pineapple balance each other perfectly.

MAKES ABOUT
· 1 ·
QUART

1 quart (1¼ pounds) strawberries, hulled and quartered

1 cup sugar

1 cup diced pineapple

½ cup freshly squeezed orange juice

Juice of 1 small lime

½ teaspoon kosher salt

In a bowl, toss together the strawberries and sugar. Allow the berries to macerate at room temperature until they release their juice, about 30 minutes.

In a blender or food processor, combine the strawberries and their juice with the pineapple, orange juice, lime juice, and salt. Puree until smooth. Pour the mixture into a bowl (if you prefer a perfectly smooth sorbet, pour the mixture through a fine-mesh strainer set over the bowl), cover, and refrigerate until cold, at least 2 hours or up to overnight.

Freeze and churn in an ice cream maker according to the manufacturer's instructions. For a soft consistency, serve the sorbet right away; for a firmer consistency, transfer it to a container, cover, and allow to harden in the freezer for 2 to 3 hours.

SOURSOP SORBET

Guanabana, or soursop as it's called in English, occasionally appears at Latin and Asian markets and specialty grocers. If you do happen to stumble across it, be sure to buy some for this recipe! The fruits are large and mango shaped, with a bumpy, spiny green skin. Inside is a white pulp studded with large black seeds; the flavor is sweet, with notes of pineapple and banana, and the texture is pearlike. *Guanabana* is a very popular sorbet in Mexico, and it was my dad's favorite.

This sorbet is made with the pulp as well as the seeds. If you can't find fresh soursop, look for it in cans or jars in Latin and Caribbean supermarkets. The flavor won't be as good as fresh and it won't contain seeds, but it's a reasonably good substitute. I don't recommend using soursop puree, however, as it lacks texture. See the following Note for how to use canned or jarred soursop in the recipe.

MAKES ABOUT
· 1¼ ·
QUARTS

3 cups fresh soursop pulp (from 1 large or 2 small fruits)

1 cup sugar

²⁄₃ cup water

1 tablespoon freshly squeezed lime juice

Pinch of kosher salt

Using a large knife, cut the soursop in half lengthwise. Using a spoon, scoop out the flesh and seeds into a measuring cup; you need a total of 3 cups. Discard the skin.

In a bowl, combine the soursop and sugar and mix with a wooden spoon, breaking up the fruit as much as possible. Stir in the water, lime juice, and salt. Cover and refrigerate until cold, at least 2 hours or up to overnight.

Freeze and churn in an ice cream maker according to the manufacturer's instructions. For a soft consistency, serve the sorbet right away; for a firmer consistency, transfer it to a container, cover, and allow to harden in the freezer for 2 to 3 hours.

NOTE If using canned or jarred soursop, you'll need to purchase around 2 pounds. Drain the fruit and reserve ½ cup of the syrup. Measure out 3 cups of pulp and continue as directed, adding the reserved syrup back to the fruit.

FRESH COCONUT SORBET

NIEVE DE COCO FRESCO

Out of all the places I've visited in Mexico, the states of Yucatán and Campeche have the best coconut sorbet I've ever tasted. The key is coconut milk made from fresh coconuts. When I asked local sorbet makers if they would ever use canned or packaged coconut milk, they looked at me with puzzled expressions; it's simply unheard of. This recipe was adapted from one given to me by a sweet man known as Chino who is famous for his *nieve de coco* in Campeche.

The idea of making homemade coconut milk may sound daunting, but I promise you'll be rewarded with a creamy, flavorful coconut sorbet that is unlike anything you can purchase in a store or make from canned coconut milk. When you shop for coconuts, make sure the "eyes" of the coconuts (the three dark rounds on one end) have no mold. You should also hear the liquid inside when you shake the coconut.

MAKES ABOUT
· 1 ·
QUART

2 large whole "dry" coconuts (the ones with the fibrous brown shell), rinsed

Water, as needed

1⅓ cups sugar

½ teaspoon kosher salt

Preheat the oven to 350°F.

Pull off any loose fibers from the coconuts. Fold a kitchen towel in half and set a coconut on top with the eyes facing up. With a clean screwdriver or sharp knife, pierce the eyes. Drain the water inside the coconut into a bowl. The water should smell clean and be clear; if it isn't, discard it. Pour the water through a fine-mesh strainer set over a second bowl. Repeat with the second coconut.

Set the coconuts on a baking sheet and bake until they begin to crack, about 30 minutes. Remove the coconuts from the oven and allow to cool until they can be handled comfortably. Hit the coconut along the cracks with the back of a knife, rotating the coconut after each whack, and it'll eventually come apart. Repeat with the second coconut.

With a sharp, small knife, pry the coconut meat from the shell, being careful not to take any brown bits with the white flesh. Measure the reserved coconut water and add enough water to total 4 cups. In a saucepan, combine the coconut meat and water. Bring to a simmer over medium heat, stirring occasionally and being careful not to let the mixture boil. Once simmering, remove the pan from the heat and allow to cool until warm.

In a blender, puree the coconut meat and liquid in batches until the meat is pulverized. Strain the puree through a fine-mesh strainer lined with several layers of cheesecloth, squeezing to extract as much liquid as possible. Blend the remaining coconut with some of the liquid and strain again, squeezing once more. Discard the coconut meat. You should have about 4 cups of coconut milk. Add the sugar and salt to the coconut milk and stir until the sugar dissolves. Cover and refrigerate until cold, at least 4 hours or up to overnight.

Freeze and churn in an ice cream maker according to the manufacturer's instructions. For a soft consistency, serve the sorbet right away; for a firmer consistency, transfer it to a container, cover, and allow to harden in the freezer for 2 to 3 hours.

KIWI SORBET

Most of Mexico's many *paleterías* (shops that sell colorful ice pops) also sell ice cream and sorbets. There is one near my dad's house in Mexico City that has the most amazing kiwi sorbet. The flavor is slightly tangy and the texture is almost creamy, even though their sorbet is dairy-free. Just as with many other sorbets in Mexico, the seeds are left in, as they add texture.

Use the ripest kiwis you can find because the sorbet will be too sour if the fruit is even the slightest bit underripe. To help them ripen, put the kiwis in a paper bag along with a banana, if you have one, and fold the bag shut. After a day or two, the kiwis should feel slightly softened when gently squeezed.

MAKES ABOUT
· 1 ·
QUART

2 pounds ripe green kiwis
2/3 cup sugar
1 tablespoon honey
¼ cup freshly squeezed lime juice
½ teaspoon kosher salt

Cut the kiwis in half and use a spoon to scoop the flesh out of the skins; discard the skins. Coarsely chop the flesh and put it in a blender or food processor, along with the sugar, honey, lime juice, and salt. Pulse until smooth and well blended but the seeds are still intact. Transfer the mixture to a container, cover, and refrigerate until cold, about 1 hour; do not refrigerate for longer than 1½ hours, as the mixture will begin to oxidize.

Freeze and churn in an ice cream maker according to the manufacturer's instructions. For a soft consistency, serve the sorbet right away; for a firmer consistency, transfer it to a container, cover, and allow to harden in the freezer for 2 to 3 hours.

CLASSIC
MEXICAN
ICE CREAMS

HELADOS CLÁSICOS, MEXICANOS

I n a country with regional differences in culture and cuisine and where ice cream is way of life for many, what qualifies as a "classic" flavor? It's not an easy question to answer. Ultimately, the ice creams I decided to include in this chapter are those that have been favorites for generations of Mexicans all across the country, that are regional specialties with lots of fans outside of their places of origin, or that are lesser-known regional flavors I feel are especially interesting and exciting. I wish I could have included many more, as I know I have omitted some classics, and even some of my own favorites aren't here simply because the main ingredient isn't found outside of its native region, making it practically impossible to replicate the flavor beyond that particular area. Some of these ice cream flavors, such as vanilla (page 68) and strawberry (page 72), will be familiar to you, but their preparation will likely be different from recipes you've seen in other cookbooks. You may find other flavors surprising, like avocado (page 74) and white corn (page 87), because their main ingredients are not commonly used in desserts. I assure you, though, each and every one of these ice creams is wonderful and so delicious.

For the most part, traditional Mexican ice creams, unlike French- and many American-style ice creams, don't contain eggs and are rarely custard

based. Instead, the bases are typically thickened with cornstarch, though some makers use guar gum (see page 13) as an emulsifier. Mexican ice cream is in fact closer in texture to Italian gelato than French- or American-style ice creams because it has a lower fat content and is less aerated.

The best-quality Mexican ice creams are made with raw milk from grass-fed cows; this milk gives the finished treats a rich texture and full flavor, although it's not uncommon for producers to use evaporated milk when they can't get raw milk. The bases are hand-churned in *garrafas* (see page 6), and many vendors

make only enough to sell for the day because without the stabilizing effect of cooked eggs, the ice creams don't keep well—although this is more work for sellers, it means that the ice cream you purchase is amazingly fresh. Sadly though, to cut costs, some producers use commercial bases to make their ice creams, but these can't compare to handmade ice creams. When you make these at home, the texture is best during the first few days, but if you keep it longer, simply set it out to soften a bit before digging in.

When developing these recipes, I wanted to stay true to tradition but also make the best version of each flavor,

so I call for making a custard base only when tradition dictates or when I felt the flavor would benefit from it. Because raw milk is difficult to get in some places, I sometimes use half-and-half and/or heavy cream to try to imitate the creamy mouthfeel and rich flavor of raw milk.

One of the things I love most about these classic ice creams is their pure, honest flavors. The featured ingredients—whether mamey fruit, peanuts, or Mexican chocolate—are allowed to shine, so you can taste all they have to offer without the distractions of competing flavors or textures. There is elegance—and deliciousness!—in simplicity.

CARAMELIZED MILK
ICE CREAM

Along the arches of the main square in the beautiful town of Pátzcuaro, Michoacán, you will find a stand called La Pacanda that sells some of the most amazing ice cream flavors you'll ever taste. This family business started in 1905, and this is the flavor that made it famous. Amparo Contreras is the head of the family nowadays. She is in her seventies and wakes up at 5:30 a.m. to make the fifteen or so flavors they prepare daily. She proudly talks about the craft and says that her favorite thing is to watch people's eyes roll back with delight as they take their first bite of Nevería La Pacanda's ice cream.

In Spanish, the word *pasta* means "paste," and here it refers to the consistency of the milk after it is cooked with sugar for hours in copper pots to create a thick yet light-colored *dulce de leche*. The caramelized milk flavor is very subtle, but it is the soul of this recipe.

MAKES ABOUT

· 1 ·

QUART

CARAMELIZED MILK
4 cups whole milk
1¼ cups sugar
¼ teaspoon baking soda
½ teaspoon
pure vanilla extract
Pinch of kosher salt

1¾ cups whole milk
1¼ cups heavy cream
½ teaspoon kosher salt
⅛ teaspoon
pure vanilla extract

To make the caramelized milk, in a heavy-bottomed large saucepan, stir together the milk, sugar, and baking soda. Bring to a boil over high heat, turn down the heat to maintain a simmer, and cook, stirring occasionally, until the mixture has thickened and is pale caramel in color, 1¼ to 1½ hours; stir more frequently as the mixture becomes thicker. You should have about 1 cup. Transfer to a heatproof bowl and allow to cool to room temperature. Stir in the vanilla and salt. If not using it right away, cover and refrigerate for up to 5 days.

Partially fill a large bowl with ice and water, place a medium bowl in the ice water, and set a fine-mesh strainer across the top.

In a saucepan, bring the milk and cream to a boil over medium heat. Remove from the heat, add the caramelized milk, and whisk until smooth and combined. Pour the mixture through the strainer into the

prepared bowl. Add the salt and vanilla and whisk until cool. Remove the bowl from the ice bath, cover, and refrigerate until the base is cold, at least 4 hours or up to overnight.

Whisk the base to recombine. Freeze and churn in an ice cream maker according to the manufacturer's instructions. For a soft consistency, serve the ice cream right away; for a firmer consistency, transfer it to a container, cover, and allow to harden in the freezer for 2 to 3 hours.

ROSE PETAL ICE CREAM

NIEVE DE ROSAS

This recipe was adapted from one given to me by Dinorah Allende, who owns Nieves Chagüita, a delightful *nevería* in Oaxaca's Benito Juárez Market. Using a variety of rose called *rosa de castilla* that has small but wonderfully fragrant petals, Chagüita makes one of the best rose petal ice creams in all of Mexico.

This ice cream is very simple and elegant. The toasted almonds add a lovely texture and a flavor that complements the rose petals, and I've added a hint of honey to heighten the floral flavor. It is important to get rose petals from a trusted source—try farmers' markets or small local growers—as the petals must be pesticide-free. The smaller the rose petals, the more intense the flavor. If you want a stronger rose flavor, add the rose extract.

MAKES ABOUT
· 1 ·
QUART

2 cups whole milk

4 ounces pesticide-free rose petals, washed and dried

1 cup almonds, toasted

1 cup heavy cream

3/4 cup sugar

1 1/2 tablespoons honey

1 teaspoon pure rose extract (optional)

In a heavy-bottomed saucepan, bring the milk to a boil. Remove from the heat and stir in half of the rose petals and all of the almonds. Allow to cool to room temperature.

In a blender, combine the milk mixture with the cream, sugar, honey, and rose extract. Puree until well blended, 3 to 4 minutes. Transfer to a container, cover, and refrigerate to allow the flavors to infuse, 2 to 3 hours. Pour the mixture into a fine-mesh strainer set over a bowl; discard the solids in the strainer.

Freeze and churn in an ice cream maker according to the manufacturer's instructions. Meanwhile, thinly slice the reserved rose petals (or if you prefer, leave them whole). When the ice cream has finished churning, stir in the rose petals. For a soft consistency, serve the ice cream right away; for a firmer consistency, transfer it to a container, cover, and allow to harden in the freezer for 2 to 3 hours. If the ice cream has hardened too much, allow it to thaw on the counter for a few minutes before serving.

CINNAMON-VANILLA CUSTARD ICE CREAM

NIEVE DE SORBETE

I fell in love with this ice cream the very first time I had it (I think I was about six years old). It is most commonly made in the state of Oaxaca, but it can also be found in Yucatán, Michoacán, and a few other places. Sometimes called *mantecado*, it's occasionally flavored only with cinnamon, but I prefer the version that includes a touch of vanilla. While most ice creams in Mexico are quite light in flavor and texture, *nieve de sorbete* is more like French- or American-style ice cream because it is made with egg yolks. It reminds me of cinnamon flan.

This recipe comes from a little ice cream stand called Niágara, which is nestled in the courtyard of a pretty church called La Soledad in Oaxaca. The ice cream makers were hesitant to share this recipe at first, but I eventually won them over and am excited to share it with you.

MAKES ABOUT
• 1 •
QUART

3 cups whole milk

¾ cup sugar

½ teaspoon kosher salt

2 (5-inch) pieces Mexican cinnamon, broken into small bits

6 large egg yolks

3 tablespoons cornstarch

1½ tablespoons pure vanilla extract

In a saucepan, bring the milk, sugar, salt, and cinnamon to a simmer over medium heat, stirring to dissolve the sugar. Remove from the heat and allow to steep for 1 hour.

Pour the milk through a fine-mesh strainer set over a bowl; discard the cinnamon. Return the milk to the saucepan and bring to a simmer over medium heat. Meanwhile, partially fill a large bowl with ice and water, place a medium bowl in the ice water, and set a fine-mesh strainer across the top.

In a bowl, whisk together the egg yolks and cornstarch. Once the milk reaches a simmer, gradually ladle about half of it into the egg mixture while whisking continuously. Whisk this mixture into the milk in the pan and cook, stirring continuously, until the custard begins to simmer and is thick enough to coat the back of the spoon, about 5 minutes. Pour the mixture through the strainer into the prepared

bowl. Add the vanilla and stir until to cool. Remove the bowl from the ice bath, cover, and refrigerate until the custard is cold, at least 4 hours or up to overnight.

Freeze and churn in an ice cream maker according to the manufacturer's instructions. For a soft consistency, serve the ice cream right away; for a firmer consistency, transfer it to a container, cover, and allow to harden in the freezer for 2 to 3 hours.

PEANUT ICE CREAM

At a party one night, my friend Caluche, who had had a few drinks, found out I was working on this book and he talked for an hour about an amazing peanut ice cream he had in Veracruz. He couldn't remember where the shop was located, but he did remember the flavor and texture of the *nieve de cacahuate*.

I never made it to Veracruz to search for that particular peanut ice cream, but I decided to develop a recipe based on what he had described. In my research, I found that the best ones are made with Mexican marzipan candy, a crumbly and slightly creamy peanut candy sold in disks. I had Caluche over to taste my version of peanut ice cream, which earned me a big smile and a hug of approval.

MAKES ABOUT
· 1¼ ·
QUARTS

3 cups half-and-half

10 ounces Mexican peanut marzipan (see Note)

½ cup sugar

½ teaspoon kosher salt

1 cup roasted peanuts, coarsely chopped

In a blender or food processor, combine the half-and-half, marzipan, sugar, and salt. Process until very smooth, about 30 seconds. Pour the mixture into a bowl, cover, and refrigerate until the base is cold, at least 2 hours or up to overnight.

Whisk the base to recombine. Freeze and churn in an ice cream maker according to the manufacturer's instructions. When the ice cream has finished churning, mix in the chopped peanuts. For a soft consistency, serve the ice cream right away; for a firmer consistency, transfer it to a container, cover, and allow to harden in the freezer for 2 to 3 hours.

NOTE If you can't find peanut marzipan candy, use 1 cup of smooth peanut butter.

MILK CURD ICE CREAM

HELADO DE CHONGOS

In the town of Zamora in the state of Michoacán, *chongos zamoranos*, or milk curds in a syrup scented with cinnamon, is a favorite dessert. Outside of Zamora, *chongos* are most often sold in cans, and truth be told, I was always turned off by their appearance and texture. It wasn't until I found an amazing family-owned candy business called La Esperanza while doing research for my first book, *My Sweet Mexico*, that I discovered good-quality *chongos* are in fact delicious. Still, the curds are something of an acquired taste, but the ice cream made with them—even with the canned *chongos* that I disliked as a child—is another story. It's sweet and creamy.

My friend Pili, who grew up in Zamora, took me to see an ice cream maker named Juan Manuel Terrez Gonzales who made his *helado de chongos* in his living room! I learned from him that using the syrup from the *chongos* to sweeten the ice cream is key. You can find *chongos* for sale online.

MAKES ABOUT
· 2 ·
QUARTS

4 cups half-and-half

1 (2-pound) can chongos zamoranos

¾ teaspoon ground Mexican cinnamon

½ teaspoon kosher salt

In a blender, combine the half-and-half, chongos zamoranos with their syrup, cinnamon, and salt and puree until smooth. Pour the mixture into a bowl, cover, and refrigerate until the base is cold, at least 2 hours or up to overnight.

Whisk the base to recombine. Freeze and churn in an ice cream maker according to the manufacturer's instructions. For a soft consistency, serve the ice cream right away; for a firmer consistency, transfer it to a container, cover, and allow to harden in the freezer for 2 to 3 hours.

MEXICAN CHOCOLATE ICE CREAM

HELADO DE CHOCOLATE MEXICANO

Chocolate in Mexico is mainly used for beverages, so chocolate ice cream isn't truly a classic flavor. Truth be told, I'm not a fan of chocolate ice cream, but Ian, my dear friend and fellow Mexico native, to whom I have dedicated this book, was. I have never met anyone who loved chocolate ice cream more than he did. He would call me from time to time just to tell me about his new favorite. I think he was trying to convert me.

In honor of Ian, I decided to include a recipe for Mexican chocolate ice cream. After much trial and error and efforts to recall his idea of the ultimate version, I achieved this recipe. It's rich tasting, with clear cinnamon notes and lots of chunks of chopped Mexican chocolate. I know it would've made him happy, and I happen to love it as well.

MAKES ABOUT
· 1½ ·
QUARTS

¼ cup unsweetened Dutch-process cocoa powder

3 cups half-and-half

12 ounces good-quality Mexican chocolate, chopped

6 large egg yolks

¾ cup sugar

¼ teaspoon kosher salt

1 cup heavy cream

2 teaspoons pure vanilla extract

In a saucepan, combine the cocoa powder and 1 cup of the half-and-half and set the pan over medium heat. Whisk the mixture until well combined, and then add the remaining 2 cups of half-and-half and 5 ounces of the chopped chocolate. Bring to a simmer, stirring occasionally, and cook until the chocolate has melted completely. Remove from the heat.

Partially fill a large bowl with ice and water, place a medium bowl in the ice water, and set a fine-mesh strainer across the top.

In a bowl, whisk together the egg yolks, sugar, and salt. Gradually ladle in about half of the hot half-and-half mixture while whisking continuously. Whisk this mixture into the half-and-half mixture in the pan. Cook over medium-low heat, stirring constantly with a wooden spoon or heatproof spatula, until the custard is thick enough to

coat the back of the spoon, about 5 minutes. Immediately pour the mixture through the strainer into the prepared bowl and stir in the heavy cream and vanilla. Allow to cool. Remove the bowl from the ice bath, cover, and refrigerate until the custard is cold, at least 4 hours or up to overnight.

Whisk the custard to recombine. Freeze and churn in an ice cream maker according to the manufacturer's instructions. When the ice cream has finished churning, mix in the remaining 7 ounces of chopped chocolate. For a soft consistency, serve the ice cream right away; for a firmer consistency, transfer it to a container, cover, and allow to harden in the freezer for 2 to 3 hours.

Vanilla is an important part of the history of Mexico as it is native to the land. It is a flavor derived from the pod that grows in an orchid. The word *vanilla* is actually rooted in *vaina*, which means "pod." The first people to cultivate it were the Totonacas, and when the Aztecs conquered them in the fifteenth century, they acquired the vanilla. It was then introduced to Europe by Hernán Cortés when the Spaniards conquered the Aztecs.

In early Mesoamerica, vanilla beans were used to perfume altars and the orchid flowers were used in combination with other plants and herbs to make items that protected against evil spirits. The Olmecas and Mayas used vanilla to flavor corn-based beverages, but those were used mainly for ceremonial rituals, as it was greatly valued and hard to come by.

It is said that Hernán Cortés arrived in Tenochtitlán (the Aztec capital city) in 1519 and was received by the emperor Moctezuma Xocoyotzin. There was a banquet prepared in his honor; a fellow soldier, Bernal Díaz, noticed that there was a beverage prepared for the high people in power. He approached one of the servants, who apparently told him it was "the beverage of the gods" prepared with *tlilxóchitl* (vanilla orchid) and *cacaotl* (cacao).

The history of vanilla is fascinating, and there have been several books on this specific subject. Hernán Cortés introduced it to Europe in 1520, but it wasn't until 1837 that a Belgian botanist named Charles François Antoine Morren discovered that the pods could be hand pollinated. Before then, bees were responsible for the pollination. This discovery allowed vanilla cultivation to go global.

Nowadays, vanilla is used worldwide in foods and perfumes. The vanilla from Mexico grows in a few areas, but mainly in Papantla, Veracruz, where this orchid originated. The flavor of Mexican vanilla is sweet and spiced and has notes of wood with a creaminess that is particular to these beans.

In Mexico, vanilla is cultivated in people's backyards and in more industrial spaces. In the areas where these orchids grow, you can find the extracts and beans, as well as figurines of all sorts made from the actual beans!

The process of harvesting the beans is quite fascinating and very labor-intensive. It begins with curing the beans by wrapping them in blankets and *petates* (straw mats); they are then placed in the sun or in low-fired ovens to dry. The beans are then spread in the sun to absorb the heat and later put inside wooden boxes overnight. Once they are cured, they are put on racks in a conditioned room to continue developing flavor.

In one of the places I visited, someone showed me a batch of beans that was hard to sell because the beans had crystallized sugary bits on the outside from the natural sugars of the vanilla. These are actually really good beans but simply sweeter, so if you come across any that look like this, don't panic!

Unfortunately, the harvest has been difficult in the past few years for various climatological and political reasons, but people in the area are hopeful that this is changing. The demand is very high but there is not enough supply at the moment. Most of the production goes to companies in the United States to make extract.

While you may see many people saying they are selling Mexican vanilla extract, please be wary because if it is priced too low then it is likely a rip-off. There are even vanilla beans that are from other parts of the world that are sold as though they are Mexican, so buy from a trusted source.

VANILLA ICE CREAM

HELADO DE VAINILLA

Mexican vanilla ice cream, like most Mexican ice creams, is not made with heavy cream and rarely contains eggs, so it is lighter than "premium" American-style ice creams. I find that without so much richness, the vanilla flavor is purer and more pronounced. However, if you prefer a custard-based vanilla ice cream, try Cinnamon-Vanilla Custard Ice Cream (page 60), but replace the cinnamon with 2 vanilla beans, split and scraped.

Mexican vanilla has a distinctive fruity aroma; I urge you to seek some out for this recipe, but the ice cream will still be delicious made with another type of vanilla. I use both vanilla beans and extract because each provides unique layers of wonderful flavor and fragrance.

MAKES ABOUT

· 1 ·

QUART

2 cups whole milk

1½ tablespoons cornstarch

¾ cup sugar

2 Mexican vanilla beans, split lengthwise

1 cup heavy cream

½ teaspoon pure Mexican vanilla extract

½ teaspoon kosher salt

Partially fill a large bowl with ice and water, place a medium bowl in the ice water, and set a fine-mesh strainer across the top.

In a small bowl, mix together ½ cup of the milk and the cornstarch. In a saucepan, combine the remaining 1½ cups of milk, the sugar, and the vanilla beans. Bring to a simmer over medium heat, stirring to dissolve the sugar. Stir the cornstarch mixture to recombine, then whisk it into the milk in the saucepan. Continue to cook, stirring continuously, until the mixture reaches a simmer and has thickened. Pour the mixture through the strainer into the prepared bowl. Add the cream, vanilla extract, and salt and stir until cool. Remove the bowl from the ice bath, cover, and refrigerate until the base is cold, at least 4 hours or up to overnight. Rinse and dry the vanilla beans and reserve them for another use (see Note).

Whisk the base to recombine. Freeze and churn in an ice cream maker according to the manufacturer's instructions. For a soft consistency, serve the ice cream right away; for a firmer consistency, transfer it to a container, cover, and allow to harden in the freezer for 2 to 3 hours.

NOTE Vanilla beans are pricey, so make sure you get as much use from them as possible. Rinse the pods under cold running water once you have used them and dry them on a rack until they are hard and brittle. Then you can put them in a container with sugar to flavor it, or blend the sugar and pods together in a food processor to make vanilla sugar. You can use either type of vanilla sugar to flavor drinks, cookies, jams, roasted fruits, and more.

GOAT'S MILK CARAMEL
ICE CREAM WITH PECANS

Cajeta is a sticky, sweet caramel sauce made from milk. It is very similar to dulce de leche but because the most common ones are made with goat's milk, the flavor has some grassy, acidic notes. The city of Celaya in Morelia is famous for its *cajeta*; there you can find it sold in jars as well as in wooden boxes that add their aroma to the *cajeta*.

This ice cream has a rich, creamy texture and an incredibly delicious caramel flavor with slightly tangy notes and a touch of cinnamon (which you can replace with a vanilla bean if you prefer).

MAKES ABOUT
· 1¼ ·
QUARTS

2 cups whole milk

1 cup heavy cream

¼ cup sugar

1 (5-inch) piece Mexican cinnamon

1¾ cups cajeta (page 154)

½ teaspoon kosher salt

¾ cup coarsely chopped pecans, toasted

Partially fill a large bowl with ice and water, place a medium bowl in the ice water, and set a fine-mesh strainer across the top.

In a saucepan, combine the milk, cream, sugar, and cinnamon and bring to a simmer over medium heat, stirring to dissolve the sugar. Remove from the heat and allow the flavors to infuse for 20 minutes. Remove and discard the cinnamon, add the cajeta and salt, and whisk until smooth and well incorporated. Pour the mixture through the strainer into the prepared bowl and stir until cool. Remove the bowl from the ice bath, cover, and refrigerate until the base is cold, at least 4 hours or up to overnight.

Whisk the base to recombine. Freeze and churn in an ice cream maker according to the manufacturer's instructions. When the ice cream has finished churning, mix in the pecans. For a soft consistency, serve the ice cream right away; for a firmer consistency, transfer it to a container, cover, and allow to harden in the freezer for 2 to 3 hours.

NOTE You can use store-bought *cajeta* if you're not up for making your own. Fat Toad Farm in Vermont makes a great version labeled "goat's milk caramel."

STRAWBERRIES AND CREAM ICE CREAM

HELADO DE FRESAS CON CREMA

Strawberry is a classic ice cream flavor in Mexico, but this version is a bit unusual. The base includes sour cream, and it's an ode to my mother, who often made a quick dessert by slicing strawberries, putting a few dollops of sour cream on top, and sprinkling on some sugar. There is something magical about the combination of tart sour cream, ripe strawberries, and just a touch of sugar.

I cannot overstate the importance of using very ripe strawberries, the kind with a fragrance so strong and sweet that you can practically taste the berries when you simply hold them to your nose. Another key to amazing strawberry ice cream is macerating the fruit. This has two purposes. The first is releasing the natural juices to give the ice cream a more pronounced flavor, and the second is lowering the freezing point of the bits of berry so that they don't become hard, icy chunks when frozen.

MAKES ABOUT
▪ **1¼** ▪
QUARTS

1 pound ripe strawberries, hulled and quartered

¾ cup sugar

1 vanilla bean, split lengthwise

2 cups half-and-half

1 cup sour cream

1 tablespoon light corn syrup

¼ teaspoon kosher salt

In a bowl, combine the strawberries and sugar. Using a paring knife, scrape the seeds from the vanilla bean halves and add the seeds and the pod to the berries. Toss well and allow to stand at room temperature for 1 hour, until the berries release their juice. Remove the vanilla pod, rinse, dry, and reserve for another use (see Note, page 69, for suggestions).

In a blender, combine the half-and-half, sour cream, corn syrup, and salt. Add about half of the strawberries and their juice and puree until smooth. Pour the mixture into a bowl, cover, and refrigerate until the base is cold, at least 1 hour or up to 4 hours. Cover and refrigerate the remaining berries.

NOTE If you have leftover strawberry juice, stir some into sparkling water or pour it over diced mangoes!

Whisk the base to recombine. Freeze and churn in an ice cream maker according to the manufacturer's instructions. Meanwhile, drain the reserved strawberries in a fine-mesh strainer set over a bowl; reserve the juice. When the ice cream has finished churning, mix in the drained strawberries along with 2 tablespoons of their juice. For a soft consistency, serve the ice cream right away; for a firmer consistency, transfer it to a container, cover, and allow to harden in the freezer for 2 to 3 hours.

AVOCADO ICE CREAM

HELADO DE AGUACATE

Growing up in Mexico, I ate avocados almost every day. My mom absolutely loves them, so she made sure we always had some around. While the fruits are mainly used in savory preparations, avocado ice cream is very common. Avocado's natural fat yields an ice cream with a very creamy texture, and its flavor is heightened with just a touch of citrus and salt.

For a dairy-free version, you can replace the milk with coconut milk or even water. Just make sure your avocados are fully ripe.

MAKES ABOUT
· 1¼ ·
QUARTS

3 ripe Hass avocados

2½ cups whole milk

1 tablespoon freshly squeezed lime juice

½ cup sugar

½ teaspoon kosher salt

Halve and pit the avocados and scoop the flesh into a blender. Add the milk, lime juice, sugar, and salt and puree until smooth. Pour the mixture into a bowl, cover, and refrigerate until the base is cold, about 2 hours.

Whisk the base to recombine. Freeze and churn in an ice cream maker according to the manufacturer's instructions. For a soft consistency, serve the ice cream right away; for a firmer consistency, transfer it to a container, cover, and allow to harden in the freezer for 2 to 3 hours.

NOTE Avocados are usually sold underripe. To help them ripen faster, put them in a paper bag—along with a banana, if you have one—and leave them at room temperature for a day or two.

RICE PUDDING ICE CREAM

HELADO DE ARROZ

Helado de arroz is very traditional in Mexico, and I love the bumpy, nubby texture the cooked grains give the ice cream. Rice pudding in Mexico is almost always flavored with cinnamon. Some people also add lime or orange zest, but I prefer mine with just a touch of vanilla.

I often add raisins to this ice cream, but my husband Danny despises them, so for this recipe I left them out (without raisins, this is one of his favorite ice creams). If you want, soak ²/₃ cup raisins in 1 cup warm water or brandy until the raisins are plump, then drain them and fold them in when the ice cream has finished churning.

MAKES ABOUT
• 1½ •
QUARTS

1½ cups whole milk

1 (3-inch) piece Mexican cinnamon

½ cup short-grain rice

1 vanilla bean, split lengthwise

1 cup heavy cream

¾ cup sugar

3 ounces cream cheese, at room temperature

Pinch of kosher salt

1 teaspoon ground Mexican cinnamon, plus extra for sprinkling

In a saucepan, combine the milk, cinnamon, rice, vanilla bean halves, and heavy cream. Bring to a simmer over medium heat and cook, stirring occasionally, until the rice is tender, 15 to 20 minutes. Add the sugar, cream cheese, and salt and stir until the sugar has dissolved and the cream cheese is incorporated. Remove from the heat, cover, and allow to cool until warm.

Partially fill a large bowl with ice and water and place a medium bowl in the ice water. Remove and discard the cinnamon from the rice mixture; remove the vanilla pod, rinse it well, and reserve it for another use (see Note, page 69, for suggestions). Stir in the ground cinnamon, transfer the mixture to the prepared bowl, and stir until cool. Remove the bowl from the ice bath, cover, and refrigerate until the base is cold, at least 4 hours or up to overnight.

Stir the base to recombine. Freeze and churn in an ice cream maker according to the manufacturer's instructions. For a soft consistency, serve the ice cream right away; for a firmer consistency, transfer it to a container, cover, and allow to harden in the freezer for 2 to 3 hours. Serve the ice cream sprinkled with ground Mexican cinnamon.

PECAN ICE CREAM

NIEVE DE NUEZ

Nogales, or pecan trees, grow beautifully in Oaxaca, so it's no wonder pecan ice cream is very popular and so amazingly good in that region. To guarantee freshness, many ice cream makers prefer to purchase pecans still in their shells and painstakingly shell the nuts themselves. My advice is to seek out the freshest pecans you can find and store them in the fridge or freezer to prevent them from turning rancid.

This recipe may seem too simple to be good, but the ice cream is delicious and a definite crowd-pleaser. It has lots of texture from the chopped pecans and the pecan flavor really shines.

MAKES ABOUT
· 1 ·
QUART

¾ cup pecans

2 cups whole milk

1 tablespoon cornstarch

¾ cup sugar

1 cup heavy cream

½ teaspoon
pure vanilla extract

½ teaspoon kosher salt

Preheat the oven to 350°F. Spread the pecans evenly on a baking sheet and toast, stirring occasionally, until fragrant, about 10 minutes. Allow to cool, then coarsely chop.

In a saucepan, whisk together the milk and cornstarch. Set the pan over medium heat, add the pecans and sugar, and cook, stirring continuously, until the mixture reaches a simmer and has fully thickened, about 7 minutes. Remove from the heat and stir in the cream, vanilla, and salt. Pour the mixture into a bowl, cover, and refrigerate until the base is cold, at least 4 hours or up to overnight.

Whisk the base to recombine. Freeze and churn in an ice cream maker according to the manufacturer's instructions. For a soft consistency, serve the ice cream right away; for a firmer consistency, transfer it to a container, cover, and allow to harden in the freezer for 2 to 3 hours.

NOTE In Puebla, I sampled a tasty ice cream called *siete nueces* (Spanish for "seven nuts"). You could use this recipe to create something similar. Simply substitute a variety of other toasted nuts, such as hazelnuts, cashews, almonds, and peanuts, for some of the pecans.

TUTTI-FRUTTI ICE CREAM

HELADO DE TUTTI-FRUTTI

Tutti-frutti is Italian for "all fruits." This ice cream is loaded with chunks of different types of candied fruit—from figs to pineapple—that are common in central Mexico. At Nevería Roxy in Mexico City, however, a variety of brightly colored fruit pastes is used instead of candied fruit, so the texture is a bit softer.

My version is a light vanilla-and-orange-scented ice cream studded with both bits of fruit paste and morsels of candied fruit for lots of interesting texture and flavor. You can use any type of candied fruit you like.

MAKES ABOUT
· 1½ ·
QUARTS

1 small orange

2½ cups half-and-half

1¼ cups heavy cream

¾ cup sugar

2 tablespoons
light corn syrup

1 vanilla bean,
split lengthwise

1½ tablespoons brandy
or rum (optional)

½ cup diced guava
paste or quince paste

½ cup chopped candied
fruit (such as pineapple,
figs, and/or apricots)

¼ cup chopped pecans,
toasted (optional)

Using a vegetable peeler, remove three strips of peel from the orange. Juice the orange; set the juice aside.

In a saucepan, combine the strips of orange peel, half-and-half, cream, sugar, corn syrup, and vanilla bean halves and bring to a simmer over medium heat, stirring to dissolve the sugar. Remove from the heat, cover, and allow to infuse for 1 hour.

Remove and discard the orange peel; remove the vanilla pods, rinse, and reserve for another use (see Note, page 69, for suggestions). Pour the mixture into a bowl and stir in the orange juice and brandy. Cover and refrigerate until the base is cold, at least 4 hours or up to overnight.

Whisk the base to recombine. Freeze and churn in an ice cream maker according to the manufacturer's instructions. When the ice cream has finished churning, fold in the fruit paste, chopped candied fruit, and pecans. For a soft consistency, serve the ice cream right away; for a firmer consistency, transfer it to a container, cover, and allow to harden in the freezer for 2 to 3 hours.

BURNT MILK ICE CREAM

NIEVE DE LECHE QUEMADA

Nieve de leche quemada is the quintessential Oaxacan ice cream; if a shop runs out, it might as well close up for the day. It is traditionally paired with prickly pear sorbet and is wildly popular. It is an acquired taste, but people in Oaxaca, even kids, go crazy for it. Although there isn't much agreement about who first created this ice cream, many of the people I spoke to while doing research believe it was most likely the result of accidentally scorching raw milk during pasteurization.

The flavor of this ice cream isn't so much caramel as it is a true burnt flavor. The degree to which the milk is burned varies from maker to maker. Some say it has to be completely charred, while others argue that only slightly burnt milk is the key. But they all agreed that it is essential to use a clay pot or else the ice cream won't taste right. I found that a regular heavy-bottomed saucepan produces great-tasting results.

I tried *leche quemada* at too many shops to count, but my favorite was at Nieves Normita in Tlacolula, which has been in operation since 1813! They cook the milk to an amber color. It is that ice cream that has inspired this recipe.

MAKES ABOUT

· 1 ·

QUART

6 cups whole raw milk

1 (5-inch) piece whole Mexican cinnamon

¾ cup sugar

3 tablespoons cornstarch

Pour 3 cups of the milk into a heavy-bottomed saucepan (preferably ceramic) and add the cinnamon. Bring to a boil over medium heat and cook, adjusting the heat as needed to maintain a simmer, until the milk has reduced to about 1 cup and has a slight burnt smell, about 40 minutes. Pour the mixture through a fine-mesh strainer set over a bowl, discard the cinnamon, and allow the milk to cool to room temperature, 30 to 40 minutes.

Partially fill a large bowl with ice and water, place a medium bowl in the ice water, and set a fine-mesh strainer across the top.

Pour the remaining 3 cups milk into the saucepan and bring to a boil over medium heat.

Meanwhile, in a small bowl, mix together the sugar and cornstarch. Add this mixture to the cooled burnt milk and stir until the sugar dissolves.

When the milk in the saucepan reaches a simmer, gradually stir in the burnt-milk mixture, bring to a simmer, stirring continuously, and cook until smooth and slightly thickened, 6 to 8 minutes. Pour the mixture through the strainer into the prepared bowl and stir until cool. Remove the bowl from the ice bath, cover, and refrigerate until the base is cold, at least 4 hours or up to overnight.

Freeze and churn in an ice cream maker according to the manufacturer's instructions. For a soft consistency, serve immediately; for a firmer consistency, transfer it to a container, cover, and allow to harden in the freezer for 2 to 3 hours.

NOTE This recipe can only be made using raw milk because regular milk evaporates and won't burn, so you won't get that deep, burnt, slightly bitter flavor.

MAMEY ICE CREAM

NIEVE DE MAMEY

My dear friend Norma told me about an ice cream stand called Helados el Popo in her hometown of Texcoco, about an hour's drive from Mexico City. Norma is an amazing cook, so I knew I had to get there as soon as possible. She was so right when she said this little red cart sells some of the very best ice creams in all of Mexico! Between serving customers, the owner explained that he offers only four flavors at a time and that with the exception of *nieve de mamey*, he often changes them. He said if he runs out of mamey ice cream, he might as well go home.

Mamey is a seasonal fruit that is available from late winter to early spring. It is oval in shape, with hard brown skin, orange-pink flesh, and a large pit at the center. Its flavor is somewhat similar to pumpkin and its texture is creamy, like an avocado. Look for fruit that feels heavy for its size and is slightly soft when gently pressed; avoid ones that seem to have a gap between the skin and the flesh. This is a very quick and easy recipe, and the ice cream is best enjoyed freshly made or within a day or so.

MAKES ABOUT
· 1 ·
QUART

2 small mamey fruits
1½ cups half-and-half
1 tablespoon light corn syrup
2/3 cup sugar
Pinch of kosher salt

Cut each mamey in half lengthwise. Discard the seed, then scoop the pulp into a blender. Add the half-and-half, corn syrup, sugar, and salt and puree until smooth. Pour the mixture into a bowl, cover, and refrigerate until the base is cold, at least 1 hour or up to 3 hours.

Whisk the base to recombine. Freeze and churn in an ice cream maker according to the manufacturer's instructions. For a soft consistency, serve the ice cream right away; for a firmer consistency, transfer it to a container, cover, and allow to harden in the freezer for 2 to 3 hours.

NOTE If you cannot find fresh mamey fruit, look for frozen mamey puree. You will need 2½ cups.

CHEESE ICE CREAM WITH BLACKBERRIES

HELADO DE QUESO CON ZARZAMORAS

MAKES ABOUT
· **1¼** ·
QUARTS

2 cups blackberries,
fresh or frozen

3 tablespoons
confectioners' sugar

2 tablespoons water

4 ounces cream cheese,
softened

6 ounces requesón
or queso fresco
(see page 16)

1½ cups half-and-half

½ cup granulated sugar

½ teaspoon
pure vanilla extract

⅛ teaspoon kosher salt

3 tablespoons
light corn syrup

1 cup heavy cream

In Mexico, *helado de queso* is usually made with only one kind of fresh cheese, *requesón*, without any other featured ingredients, so the cheese flavor really shines. I absolutely love it, especially when there are a few chunks of cheese to bite into. The texture of this ice cream can be slightly grainy due to the cheese, but it's truly fantastic.

Occasionally, you will find *helado de queso* with fruit mixed in, whether bits of fresh fruit, a jamlike concoction, or fruit paste. The combination is delicious and reminds me of a sort of cheesecake (in fact, feel free to add some crushed Maria cookies to turn it into a cheesecake ice cream). My favorite combination with this ice cream is to pair it with a scoop of Mixed Berries Sorbet (page 41).

In a saucepan, combine the blackberries, confectioners' sugar, and water. Set the pan over low heat and cook, stirring frequently, until the mixture comes to a boil. Cook for 2 minutes, until it has thickened slightly, then transfer to a bowl. Gently mash the berries with the back of a spoon, cover, and refrigerate until ready to use.

In a blender or food processor, combine the cream cheese, 3 ounces of the requesón, the half-and-half, granulated sugar, vanilla, salt, and corn syrup. Puree until smooth. Transfer to a bowl and add the cream and the remaining 3 ounces of requesón. Whisk gently to combine; the mixture should be slightly chunky. Cover and refrigerate until the base is cold, at least 2 hours or up to overnight.

. . . CONTINUED

CLASSIC MEXICAN ICE CREAMS

CHEESE
ICE CREAM
WITH
BLACKBERRIES
CONTINUED

Whisk the base to recombine. Freeze and churn in an ice cream maker according to the manufacturer's instructions. When the ice cream has finished churning, mix in the chilled blackberries. For a soft consistency, serve the ice cream right away; for a firmer consistency, transfer it to a container, cover, and allow to harden in the freezer for 2 to 3 hours.

NOTE The two Mexican cheeses most commonly found in the United States are *requesón* and *queso fresco*. You can use either one, but *queso fresco* yields a slightly saltier ice cream.

MEXICAN ICE CREAM

WHITE CORN ICE CREAM

NIEVE DE ELOTE

Corn is at the heart of Mexican cuisine and is used in all sorts of savory and sweet preparations. In Mexico, white corn is the one used most commonly for ice cream, but the variety used isn't sweet like the corn sold in grocery stores in the United States. You can occasionally find it frozen or in farmers' markets. However, if you can only find sweet corn, you can definitely use it, but reduce the sugar to 2/3 cup and use only 1 tablespoon of corn syrup.

This ice cream has a lot of texture and deep corn flavor. Try it with a bit of salted chile on top the way they do in many places.

MAKES ABOUT

· 1 ·

QUART

2 cups whole milk

2 tablespoons cornstarch

2 ears fresh corn, not sweet and preferably white, shucked

1½ cups heavy cream

¾ cup sugar

2 tablespoons light corn syrup

½ teaspoon kosher salt

½ teaspoon pure vanilla extract

In a small bowl, whisk together ¼ cup of the milk and the cornstarch. Set aside.

Using a chef's knife, cut the corn kernels from the cobs, then cut each cob crosswise into 2 or 3 pieces. In a large saucepan, combine the corn kernels and cobs, the remaining 1¾ cups of milk, and the cream, sugar, corn syrup, and salt. Bring to a simmer over medium heat, stirring to dissolve the sugar, then adjust the heat to maintain a gentle simmer. Stir the cornstarch mixture to recombine, then stir it into the corn mixture. Cook, stirring continuously, until the mixture returns to a simmer and has thickened slightly, about 6 minutes. Remove from the heat and stir in the vanilla. Cover and allow to steep for 2 hours.

Remove and discard the corn cobs. Transfer 1½ cups of the mixture to a blender and puree until smooth. Return the pureed portion to the rest of the mixture, then transfer the mixture to a bowl. Cover and refrigerate until the base is cold, at least 4 hours or up to overnight.

Whisk the base to recombine. Freeze and churn in an ice cream maker according to the manufacturer's instructions. For a soft consistency, serve the ice cream right away; for a firmer consistency, transfer it to a container, cover, and allow to harden in the freezer for 2 to 3 hours.

MODERN
MEXICAN
ICE CREAMS

HELADOS DEL MÉXICO MODERNO

Among the many family-owned ice cream businesses that are handed down from generation to generation and that continue the quality and rich traditions that make Mexican ice cream so special, there are countless innovators who are trying to appeal to customers' changing tastes and sense of adventure. This chapter is focused on those modern and inventive takes on Mexican ice cream and on new interpretations of classic flavors.

Xochimilco, on the outskirts of Mexico City, hosts an annual ice cream festival where you'll find so many outrageous flavors: lettuce, shrimp, snake, chorizo, and even Viagra! But I believe most of these are produced just for shock value and aren't really meant to be enjoyed. In my research, however, I met ice cream makers who create unusual flavors and who are very serious about their craft. Eugenio Aguilar, owner of Helados Aguilar in Dolores Hidalgo, churns out classic *nieves* such as cola while also offering edgy flavors that challenge his customers' palates. For inspiration, he turns to traditional Mexican cuisine and makes savory-themed ice creams such as black bean, shrimp cocktail with cactus, *chicharrón* (complete with bits of pork rind!), and his personal favorite, *chile relleno.* To be honest, I am not particularly fond of these flavors, but there is no denying that the quality of his ice cream is

top-notch, and I greatly admire Eugenio's passion, dedication, and creativity.

Even some of the oldest ice cream establishments in Mexico are becoming innovative in order to stay competitive, as there are many new shops offering novel, trendy flavors to draw in customers. In Mexico City, La Especial de Paris, which has been around for almost a century, has always been famous for classic *nieves* such as coconut, orange, and pineapple, but Vicente Lozada, the current owner, feels that evolving with the times is essential for staying in business. When he introduced ice creams like olive oil

with cranberries and black cardamom and tobacco, he found a new, younger, and more adventurous customer base. I believe that what makes shops such as La Especial de Paris different from—and better than—many of the new "cooler" competitors is the high quality of the ingredients used in the *nieves* and *helados*, as well as the care and commitment that go into making them the right way. Fortunately for all ice cream lovers, artisans like Eugenio Aguilar are keeping Mexico's ice cream making traditions alive, and in the process creating new classics.

Just in case you're wondering what kinds of recipes are in this chapter, not all modern Mexican ice cream flavors feature out-there ingredients or wild combinations. Most of the recipes I included are crowd-pleasers—what's not to love about Horchata Ice Cream (page 93) or Lime Gelato with Chia Seeds (page 101)? What makes them "modern" is that they are simply not considered classics in Mexico. Many were flavors that I encountered during my research, and a few I created on my own, based on ingredients and combinations that remind me of home.

HORCHATA ICE CREAM

Horchata is a traditional Mexican drink made with grains, spices, and sometimes nuts. There are many different versions, but the most common is made with rice and Mexican cinnamon. I think the addition of almonds is especially good because nuts add a rich, full flavor. *Horchata* is my sister's favorite *agua fresca*, so she would definitely approve of this version turned into ice cream.

Toasting the rice, cinnamon, and almonds really enhances their flavors. The starch from the rice adds a certain richness to this ice cream and makes it quite addictive.

MAKES ABOUT
· 1 ·
QUART

1/3 cup almonds

1/3 cup long-grain rice

1 (3-inch) piece Mexican cinnamon

4 cups half-and-half

5 large egg yolks

3/4 cup sugar

3/4 teaspoon kosher salt

1/4 teaspoon pure vanilla extract

Ground Mexican cinnamon, for sprinkling

In a large saucepan, toast the almonds, rice, and cinnamon over medium heat, stirring frequently, until the almonds are slightly golden and the cinnamon is very fragrant, 3 to 4 minutes. Add the half-and-half, stir to combine, and bring to a simmer. Remove from the heat, cover, and allow to steep for 2 hours.

In a blender, working in two batches, puree the almond mixture until the nuts are pulverized and resemble a coarse flour. Pour each batch through a fine-mesh strainer set over a bowl and press down on the solids with a spatula or spoon to extract as much liquid as possible; discard the solids in the strainer. Blend the liquid in batches and strain once more; discard any solids left in the strainer.

Partially fill a large bowl with ice and water, place a medium bowl in the ice water, and set the fine-mesh strainer across the top.

Return the strained liquid to the saucepan and bring to a simmer over medium heat. Meanwhile, in a heatproof bowl, whisk together the egg yolks and sugar. Gradually ladle in about half of the hot liquid while whisking continuously. Whisk this mixture into the liquid in

. . . CONTINUED

the saucepan and cook, stirring continuously, until the custard is thick enough to coat the back of the spoon. Pour the custard through the strainer into the prepared bowl, add the salt and vanilla, and stir until cool. Remove the bowl from the ice bath, cover, and refrigerate until the custard is cold, at least 3 hours or up to overnight.

Whisk the custard to recombine. Freeze and churn in an ice cream maker according to the manufacturer's instructions. For a soft consistency, serve the ice cream right away; for a firmer consistency, transfer it to a container, cover, and allow to harden in the freezer for 2 to 3 hours. Serve the ice cream sprinkled with ground Mexican cinnamon.

WALNUT ICE CREAM WITH POMEGRANATE

HELADO DE NOGADA

Chiles en nogada is a dish traditionally prepared during Mexican Independence festivities in September. Roasted poblano chiles are filled with a spiced meat-and-fruit mixture and topped with a creamy walnut sauce called *nogada* before being sprinkled with pomegranate seeds. The dish, created in honor of emperor Agustín de Iturbide, who led Mexico in its fight for independence from Spain, is a delicious display of the colors of the Mexican flag: red, white, and green.

At Heladería Delizzia Gourmet in Puebla, I tasted *helado de nogada*, an ice cream inspired by *chiles en nogada*. It was truly fantastic—and only available for a limited time, so I was fortunate to have the chance to try it! I created this recipe based on that *helado de nogada*, and I make it only during the month of September, to celebrate Mexican independence.

MAKES ABOUT
· 1 ·
QUART

1 tablespoon cornstarch

2 cups whole milk

1 cup heavy cream

¾ cup sugar

½ teaspoon kosher salt

4 ounces soft goat cheese, crumbled

2 ounces cream cheese, softened

1½ cups walnuts, soaked in water or frozen to keep from turning brown

½ teaspoon ground Mexican cinnamon

2 tablespoons sherry

1 cup pomegranate seeds

Partially fill a large bowl with ice and water, place a medium bowl in the ice water, and set a fine-mesh strainer across the top.

In a small bowl, whisk together the cornstarch and ¼ cup of the milk.

In a saucepan, combine the remaining 1¾ cups of milk with the cream, sugar, and salt and bring to a simmer over medium heat, stirring occasionally. Stir the cornstarch mixture to recombine and stir it into the milk mixture. Cook, stirring continuously, until the mixture returns to a simmer and has thickened slightly, about 6 minutes. Remove from the heat, add the goat cheese and cream cheese, and whisk until smooth. Pour the mixture through the strainer into the prepared bowl and stir until cool.

. . . CONTINUED

WALNUT ICE CREAM WITH POMEGRANATE

CONTINUED

In a blender, working in two batches, puree the cooled milk mixture and the walnuts until the nuts are pulverized (some small bits may remain), 4 to 5 minutes. Transfer to a bowl and stir in the cinnamon and sherry. Cover and refrigerate until cold, at least 2 hours or up to 4 hours.

Freeze and churn in an ice cream maker according to the manufacturer's instructions. When the ice cream has finished churning, mix in the pomegranate seeds. For a soft consistency, serve the ice cream right away; for a firmer consistency, transfer it to a container, cover, and allow to harden in the freezer for 2 to 3 hours.

CHOCOLATE ICE CREAM WITH PEANUT MARZIPAN

HELADO DE CHOCOLATE CON MAZAPÁN

When I was a kid, one of my favorite candies (and one of the few my mom allowed me to have) was *mazapán*, crumbly peanut confections sold on street corners and in bodega-type shops. The texture and flavor are somewhere between peanut butter and a crumbly buttery cookie. Sadly, I later became mildly allergic to peanuts, so I don't get to enjoy them anymore.

While doing research for this book, my friend Gus and I visited Heladería Delizzia Gourmet in Puebla. We were sampling lots of flavors, and he stuck a spoonful of ice cream in my mouth saying I had to try it! The flavor was rich, dark chocolate, and I tasted delicious bits of the *mazapán* that I loved so much as a child. I wasn't thinking about how sick I'd be but rather how happy and nostalgic I felt. I knew I had to include this recipe in the book, so here is my version. Use high-quality bittersweet chocolate and cocoa, as they make all the difference.

MAKES ABOUT
• 1½ •
QUARTS

⅔ cup crumbled peanut marzipan (about 10 individual pieces)

7½ ounces bittersweet chocolate, finely chopped

3 cups half-and-half

½ cup sugar

6 large egg yolks

3½ tablespoons unsweetened Dutch-process cocoa powder, sifted

2 teaspoons ground Mexican cinnamon (optional)

1 teaspoon kosher salt

In a small bowl, freeze the peanut marzipan until needed.

Put the chocolate in a large heatproof bowl, set a fine-mesh strainer across the top, and set the bowl in a larger bowl of ice water.

In a saucepan, combine the half-and-half with about half of the sugar. Bring to a simmer over medium heat, stirring to dissolve the sugar.

Meanwhile, in a heatproof bowl, whisk the egg yolks, remaining sugar, cocoa powder, cinnamon, and salt until well incorporated and lump-free. Gradually ladle about half of the hot half-and-half mixture into the egg yolks while whisking continuously, then whisk

. . . CONTINUED

MODERN MEXICAN ICE CREAMS

this mixture into the half-and-half in the saucepan. Cook, stirring continuously, until the custard is thick enough to coat the back of the spoon. Pour the custard through the strainer into the bowl with the chocolate and whisk until the chocolate has completely melted and the mixture is cool. Remove the bowl from the ice bath, cover, and refrigerate until the custard is cold, at least 2 hours or up to 6 hours.

Freeze and churn in an ice cream maker according to the manufacturer's instructions. When the ice cream has finished churning, mix in the marzipan pieces. For a soft consistency, serve the ice cream right away; for a firmer consistency, transfer it to a container, cover, and allow to harden in the freezer for 2 to 3 hours.

LIME GELATO
WITH CHIA SEEDS

GELATO DE LIMÓN CON CHIA

MAKES ABOUT
· 1¼ ·
QUARTS

At La Newyorkina, we make a lime-chia ice cream inspired by lime-chia *agua fresca*, one of my all-time favorite beverages. (Lime-chia *agua fresca* has been around since long before chia seeds became trendy.)

I love the combination of lime and cream because the fruit's acidity and the dairy's richness balance each other out, so the flavor is still fresh and bright but the consistency is nice and creamy. The chia seeds add a really nice texture and give the ice cream a unique appearance, too.

Grated zest and juice of 4 limes

¾ cup sugar

2 cups half-and-half

5 large egg yolks

1¼ cups heavy cream

⅔ cup chia seeds

In a food processor, pulse the lime zest and sugar about 5 times to extract the oils from the zest. Transfer the lime sugar to a bowl.

Partially fill a large bowl with ice and water, place a medium bowl in the ice water, and set a fine-mesh strainer across the top.

In a saucepan, combine ½ cup of the lime sugar and the half-and-half. Bring to a simmer over medium heat, stirring to dissolve the sugar. Meanwhile, add the egg yolks to the remaining lime sugar in the bowl and whisk to combine. Gradually ladle about half of the hot half-and-half mixture into the yolks while whisking continuously, then whisk this mixture into the half-and-half in the saucepan. Cook, stirring continuously, until the custard is thick enough to coat the back of the spoon, about 5 minutes. Pour the custard through the strainer into the prepared bowl and stir until cool. Stir in the lime juice, cream, and chia seeds. Remove the bowl from the ice bath, cover, and refrigerate until the custard is cold, at least 2 hours or up to 4 hours.

Freeze and churn in an ice cream maker according to the manufacturer's instructions. For a soft consistency, serve the ice cream right away; for a firmer consistency, transfer it to a container, cover, and allow to harden in the freezer for 2 to 3 hours.

MODERN MEXICAN ICE CREAMS

TAMARIND-CHILE SORBET WITH GRASSHOPPERS

NIEVE DE TAMARINDO CON CHILE Y CHAPULINES

In Oaxaca, fried grasshoppers tossed with salt, chile, and lime are sold in markets and on the street for enjoying as a snack. They are crunchy, slightly salty, and spicy, with—not surprisingly—grassy notes. I absolutely love them!

I tried this sorbet at Manolo Nieves in Oaxaca thinking it was just a gimmicky flavor, but it was delicious, and I had to include the recipe in this book. The sweet-and-sour flavor of the tamarind, the heat from the chile, and the saltiness of the crunchy grasshoppers complement each other so well.

MAKES ABOUT

• 1 •

QUART

1¼ pounds tamarind pods (see page 16), or 1 pound tamarind pulp with seeds

1¼ cups sugar

2 tablespoons light corn syrup

2 teaspoons ground piquín or árbol chile, or cayenne pepper

¾ cup dried or fried grasshoppers with chile

If using tamarind pods, peel them, discarding the hard shell, and soak the fruit in hot water until soft, 1 to 2 hours. Strain the softened tamarind through a fine-mesh strainer set over a large bowl, pressing on the solids with the back of a wooden spoon to extract as much liquid and pulp as possible. You should have about 1 cup of strained pulp.

In a saucepan, combine 3 cups of water, the sugar, and the corn syrup. Bring to a simmer over medium heat, stirring to dissolve the sugar. Pour the syrup into the strained tamarind pulp, add the chile, and whisk until well combined. If you used the tamarind pulp instead of the pods, remove the seeds from the mixture using a fine-mesh strainer. Cover and refrigerate until cold, at least 2 hours or up to overnight.

Freeze and churn in an ice cream maker according to the manufacturer's instructions. When the sorbet has finished churning, gently mix in the grasshoppers, reserving some for garnish if you like. For a soft consistency, serve the sorbet right away; for a firmer consistency, transfer it to a container, cover, and allow to harden in the freezer for 2 to 3 hours.

NOTE Dried and fried grasshoppers are not easy to find but there are specialty Mexican stores that sell them. If you know someone going to Oaxaca, make sure they bring some back for you. You can also purchase them online or sometimes at Mexican restaurants.

MALT ICE CREAM

HELADO DE MALTA

At the back of the Mercado de Medellín in Mexico City is an ice cream stand called Helados Palmeiro. The stand displays a sign reading HELADOS CUBANOS (Cuban ice cream) and, underneath, HELADOS DE CREMA DE LECHE, which basically indicates that the ice cream sold there is creamier than traditional Mexican ice cream. The owner, Eugenio Palmeiro Rios, is a fascinating man. Originally from Cuba, he has a master's degree in chemistry but became a molecular biologist. Disappointed with Mexican ice cream, he started making his own, using his background in science as he developed his recipes. It is now his full-time business and he has become a bit of a legend.

Of all of Eugenio's *helados Cubanos*, this malt ice cream was my favorite. It's rich and creamy, and the malt flavor is irresistible.

MAKES ABOUT
· 1 ·
QUART

1 cup whole milk

¾ cup sugar

6 large egg yolks

2 cups heavy cream

¾ cup malted milk powder

½ teaspoon kosher salt

¼ teaspoon pure vanilla extract

Partially fill a large bowl with ice and water, place a medium bowl in the ice water, and set a fine-mesh strainer across the top.

In a saucepan, combine the milk and about half of the sugar. Bring to a simmer over medium heat, stirring occasionally to dissolve the sugar. Meanwhile, in a heatproof bowl, whisk together the egg yolks and the remaining sugar. Gradually ladle about half of the hot milk into the yolk mixture, whisking continuously. Whisk this mixture into the milk in the saucepan and cook, stirring constantly, until the custard is thick enough to coat the back of the spoon, 5 to 7 minutes. Pour the custard through the strainer into the prepared bowl. Whisk in the cream, malt powder, salt, and vanilla and stir until the custard is cool. Remove the bowl from the ice bath, cover, and refrigerate until the custard is cold, at least 2 hours or up to overnight.

Freeze and churn in an ice cream maker according to the manufacturer's instructions. For a soft consistency, serve the ice cream immediately; for a firmer consistency, transfer it to a container, cover, and allow to harden in the freezer for 2 to 3 hours.

TANGERINE ICE CREAM

HELADO DE MANDARINA

One of the most inspiring people I met during my research was Normita. She owns a shop in Oaxaca bearing her name, Nevería Normita, that her great-grandfather opened in 1813! With a deep curiosity and desire for knowledge, she is one of those people you are immediately drawn to and could talk with for hours on end.

To make the amazing tangerine ice cream that she sells at her shop, Normita uses the fruit from the tangerine tree in the courtyard behind her house. The flavor is fresh and bright, but the milk gives it a bit of richness and tames the acidity of the fruit. It reminds me of a Creamsicle but tastes way better.

MAKES ABOUT

· 1 ·

QUART

1½ cups whole milk

½ cup sugar

¼ teaspoon kosher salt

¼ cup grated
tangerine zest

1½ cups freshly
squeezed tangerine juice

½ teaspoon
pure vanilla extract

⅓ cup light corn syrup

In a blender, combine all of the ingredients and puree until the sugar dissolves, 3 to 4 minutes. Pour the mixture into a container, cover, and refrigerate until the base is cold, at least 1 hour or up to 4 hours.

Whisk the base to recombine. Freeze and churn in an ice cream maker according to the manufacturer's instructions. For a soft consistency, serve the ice cream right away; for a firmer consistency, transfer it to a container, cover, and allow to harden in the freezer for 2 to 3 hours.

GOAT CHEESE AND HOJA SANTA ICE CREAM

NIEVE DE QUESO DE CABRA Y HOJA SANTA

Hoja santa is an herb with an anise-like flavor. The name translates to "sacred plant," and the beautiful heart-shaped leaves are large and broad. It is most often used in traditional savory dishes.

This ice cream was inspired by one that I tried at Helados Manolo, a fifth-generation family-owned business in Oaxaca. I was surprised that this flavor was my dad's favorite. The flavor is not exactly savory, but the goat cheese and *hoja santa* make this an unusual combination.

MAKES ABOUT

• 1 •

QUART

6 ounces fresh goat cheese, crumbled

4 ounces fresh hoja santa

2 cups whole milk

1¼ cups heavy cream

3 tablespoons honey

½ teaspoon kosher salt

4 large egg yolks

½ cup sugar

NOTE You can find hoja santa at Latin markets.

Put 4 ounces of the goat cheese and 2 ounces of the hoja santa in a medium heatproof bowl, set a fine-mesh strainer across the top, and set the bowl in a larger bowl partially filled with ice and water.

Combine the milk, cream, honey, and salt in a saucepan and bring to a simmer over medium heat, stirring to dissolve the honey. Meanwhile, in a heatproof bowl, whisk together the egg yolks and sugar. Gradually ladle in about half of the hot milk mixture while whisking continuously. Whisk this mixture into the liquid in the saucepan and cook, stirring continuously, until the custard is thick enough to coat the back of the spoon. Pour the custard through the strainer onto the goat cheese and hoja santa and whisk until the cheese is melted and the mixture is cool; discard the hoja santa in the strainer. In a blender, pulse the reserved 2 ounces of hoja santa 3 or 4 times. Mix the pulsed hoja santa into the custard. Remove the bowl from the ice bath, cover, and refrigerate until the custard is cold, at least 4 hours or up to overnight.

Freeze and churn in an ice cream maker according to the manufacturer's instructions. Stir in the remaining 2 ounces of goat cheese. Transfer to a container and allow to harden in the freezer for 2 to 3 hours.

LIME PIE ICE CREAM

HELADO DE PAY DE LIMÓN

I am not sure when this flavor became so popular in Mexico, but it is definitely a twist on American Key lime pie. It's so simple to make but tastes oh so good! The ice cream has a wonderfully creamy texture, a bright lime flavor, and a pleasing crunch from the crushed cookies. It is very important to use fresh limes in this recipe. Bottled juice just can't compare.

MAKES ABOUT
· 1¼ ·
QUARTS

3 cups coarsely crushed Maria cookies or graham crackers

1 (14-ounce) can sweetened condensed milk

1½ cups half-and-half

1 tablespoon grated lime zest

¾ cup freshly squeezed lime juice

½ teaspoon kosher salt

Put the crushed cookies in a small bowl and freeze until needed.

In a bowl, whisk together the sweetened condensed milk, half-and-half, lime zest, lime juice, and salt until thoroughly combined. Cover and refrigerate until cold, at least 2 hours or up to overnight.

Freeze and churn in an ice cream maker according to the manufacturer's instructions. When the ice cream has finished churning, mix in the crushed cookies. For a soft consistency, serve the ice cream right away; for a firmer consistency, transfer it to a container, cover, and allow to harden in the freezer for 2 to 3 hours.

NOTE Maria cookies are lightly sweetened vanilla-flavored cookies. If you can't find them, graham crackers make an equally delicious substitution.

NESCAFÉ ICE CREAM

NIEVE DE NESCAFÉ

MAKES ABOUT
· 1 ·
QUART

Although there are many different brands of instant coffee, Nescafé is the one that dominates the Mexican market, and in many households, it is the only coffee that's served. So it's no surprise that this ice cream flavor is so popular—and that it actually goes by the name *nieve de Nescafé*. ("Instant coffee ice cream" just doesn't sound the same.) Like many *nieves* in Mexico, this ice cream is made with milk, not cream, and is thickened with a bit of cornstarch instead of eggs, so the mouthfeel isn't heavy or too rich.

3 cups whole milk

⅓ cup Nescafé

¾ cup sugar

3 tablespoons cornstarch

½ teaspoon pure vanilla extract

Partially fill a large bowl with ice and water, place a medium bowl in the ice water, and set a fine-mesh strainer across the top.

In a saucepan, combine 2 cups of the milk and the Nescafé. Bring to a simmer over medium heat, stirring to dissolve the coffee. Meanwhile, in a bowl, whisk together the remaining 1 cup of milk, the sugar, and the cornstarch. Gradually add the cornstarch mixture to the milk mixture in the saucepan while stirring continuously. Continue to cook, stirring, until the mixture returns to a simmer and has thickened, 5 to 7 minutes. Pour the mixture through the strainer into the prepared bowl and stir until cool. Stir in the vanilla. Remove the bowl from the ice bath, cover, and refrigerate until cold, at least 3 hours or up to overnight.

Freeze and churn in an ice cream maker according to the manufacturer's instructions. For a soft consistency, serve the ice cream right away; for a firmer consistency transfer it to a container, cover, and allow to harden in the freezer for 2 to 3 hours.

MODERN MEXICAN ICE CREAMS

TRES LECHES ICE CREAM

HELADO DE TRES LECHES

Tres leches translates as "three milks," and it's the name of a special-occasion Latin American dessert that's becoming more and more popular in the United States: vanilla sponge cake soaked with a mixture of three different types of milk (evaporated milk, sweetened condensed milk, and cream).

Tres leches ice cream was one of first flavors I developed for La Newyorkina, and it quickly became a signature flavor and favorite in the kitchen. To make this recipe, you'll have to bake a cake, cut it into cubes, and freeze the cubes, but this can all be done ahead of time. This ice cream is itself a reason for celebration!

MAKES ABOUT
· 1 ·
QUART

CAKE

½ cup unbleached
all-purpose flour

¾ teaspoon
baking powder

Pinch of kosher salt

3 large eggs, separated,
at room temperature

½ cup sugar

3 tablespoons
whole milk

¼ teaspoon
pure vanilla extract

To make the cake, position a rack in the center of the oven and preheat the oven to 350°F. Butter the bottom and sides of a 9-inch square baking pan. Line the bottom with parchment paper and lightly butter the parchment paper.

In a bowl, whisk together the flour, baking powder, and salt. Sift this mixture into a second bowl and set aside.

In a large bowl, combine the egg yolks and ¼ cup of the sugar. Using an electric mixer, beat the mixture until it is pale and creamy, about 5 minutes. Add the milk and vanilla and beat until combined, about 1 minute more. Clean and dry the beaters.

In another large bowl, beat the egg whites on low speed until foamy, then continue to beat, gradually increasing the speed to high, until the egg whites hold soft peaks when the beaters are lifted, 2 to 3 minutes. Continue to beat on high speed while gradually adding the remaining ¼ cup of sugar; stop when the egg whites hold stiff peaks and before they begin to look dry and lumpy.

. . . CONTINUED

MODERN MEXICAN ICE CREAMS

ICE CREAM BASE

1 (12-ounce) can evaporated milk

1 (14-ounce) can sweetened condensed milk

1½ cups half-and-half

¾ teaspoon pure vanilla extract

½ teaspoon salt

Whisk one-third of the flour mixture into the yolk mixture until thoroughly combined. Using a rubber spatula, gently fold in one-third of the egg whites. Alternate folding in the remaining flour mixture and the remaining egg whites in a total of four additions. Pour the batter into the prepared pan and bake until a toothpick inserted into the center comes out clean, about 20 minutes.

Allow the cake to cool in the pan on a wire rack for 10 minutes, then invert it onto the rack, remove the parchment paper, and allow to cool to room temperature. Cut the cake into 1-inch cubes and freeze on a sheet pan until ready to use. (If you'd prefer the cake cubes to have a bit of crunch in the ice cream, before freezing, toast them on the sheet pan at 350°F for about 6 minutes, until golden brown.)

To make the ice cream base, in a bowl, whisk all of the ingredients until well combined. Cover and refrigerate until cold, at least 1 hour or up to overnight.

Freeze and churn in an ice cream maker according to the manufacturer's instructions. When the ice cream has finished churning, mix in the frozen cake pieces. For a soft consistency, serve the ice cream right away; for a firmer consistency, transfer it to a container, cover, and allow to harden in the freezer for 2 to 3 hours.

NOTE You can make this into coconut tres leches ice cream by using 12 ounces unsweetened coconut milk in place of the evaporated milk and mixing 1 cup toasted shredded coconut into the churned ice cream along with the bits of cake.

MEXICAN ICE CREAM

COFFEE-CAJETA ICE CREAM WITH MEXICAN CHOCOLATE

HELADO DE CAFÉ CON CAJETA Y CHOCOLATE

My dear friend Nick loves ice cream more than anyone I know. When he lived in New York, he would come over to my apartment several times a week to hang out, and he almost always showed up with a pint of ice cream. I wanted to create a flavor in his honor, so I combined a few of his favorite ingredients—deep, dark coffee; rich *cajeta* (goat's milk caramel); and chunks of Mexican chocolate—to make this killer flavor. Another name for it could be Nick's Dream.

MAKES ABOUT
· 1 ·
QUART

2 cups heavy cream

1 cup half-and-half

¾ cup sugar

6 large egg yolks

6 tablespoons medium-grind coffee, preferably Mexican

1 teaspoon pure vanilla extract

½ teaspoon kosher salt

⅔ cup cajeta (page 154)

5 ounces good-quality Mexican chocolate, chopped

Partially fill a large bowl with ice and water, place a medium bowl in the ice water, and set a fine-mesh strainer across the top.

In a saucepan, combine the cream, half-and-half, and about half of the sugar. Bring to simmer over medium heat, stirring to dissolve the sugar. Meanwhile, in a bowl, whisk together the egg yolks, the remaining sugar, and the coffee. Gradually ladle about ½ cup of the hot cream mixture into the egg yolk mixture while whisking continuously. Whisk this mixture into the saucepan and cook, stirring continuously, until the custard is thick enough to coat the back of the spoon, 2 to 3 minutes. Pour the custard through the strainer into the prepared bowl and stir until cool. Stir in the vanilla and salt. Remove the bowl from the ice bath, cover, and refrigerate until the custard is cold, at least 4 hours or up to overnight.

Whisk the custard to recombine. Freeze and churn in an ice cream maker according to the manufacturer's instructions. When the ice cream has finished churning, mix in the cajeta and chopped chocolate. For a soft consistency, serve the ice cream right away; for a firmer consistency, transfer it to a container, cover, and allow to harden in the freezer for 2 to 3 hours.

MEXICAN PECAN PRALINE AND CINNAMON ICE CREAM

HELADO DE PRALINÉ DE NUEZ CON CANELA

A few years ago, Jessica B. Harris, PhD, author, journalist, and professor, invited me to speak at a praline colloquium in New Orleans. I was amazed at the diversity of praline culture within the South, and I even heard about a Mexican praline ice cream that Blue Bell makes. We don't call them pralines in Mexico for the most part, but we do have similar confections made from caramel and pecans.

In this recipe, a custard base yields a rich, creamy ice cream; the Mexican cinnamon brings its unique fragrance and flavor notes; and the crunchy, sweet pecans add terrific texture. This is one that's hard to stop eating!

MAKES ABOUT
· 1¼ ·
QUARTS

PECAN PRALINES
1 cup packed dark brown sugar

½ cup granulated sugar

½ cup heavy cream

4 tablespoons unsalted butter

½ teaspoon kosher salt

¾ teaspoon ground Mexican cinnamon

2 tablespoons water

1 cup pecan halves

To make the pecan pralines, line a baking sheet with parchment paper.

In a heavy-bottomed saucepan, combine the brown sugar, granulated sugar, cream, butter, salt, cinnamon, and water. Set the pan over medium heat and cook, stirring constantly, until the mixture reaches 238°F to 240°F on a candy thermometer. Remove the saucepan from the heat, add the pecans, and stir vigorously but carefully with a wooden spoon or heatproof spatula until the pecans are evenly coated with the caramel. Pour the mixture onto the prepared baking sheet and allow to cool. Once cool, break the praline into bite-size pieces by coarsely chopping it with a knife or by whacking it lightly with a rolling pin. Store in an airtight container until ready to use.

ICE CREAM BASE

1½ cups heavy cream

1 cup whole milk

1 (3-inch) piece
Mexican cinnamon

2/3 cup granulated sugar

½ teaspoon kosher salt

1 teaspoon
pure vanilla extract

5 large egg yolks

To make the ice cream base, partially fill a large bowl with ice and water, place a medium bowl in the ice water, and set a fine-mesh strainer across the top.

In a saucepan, combine the cream, milk, cinnamon, about half of the granulated sugar, the salt, and the vanilla. Bring to a simmer over medium heat, stirring to dissolve the sugar. Remove from the heat.

In a bowl, whisk together the egg yolks and the remaining sugar. Gradually ladle in about ½ cup of the warm cream mixture while whisking continuously. Whisk the yolk mixture into the cream mixture in the pan and cook over medium heat, stirring continuously, until the custard is thick enough to coat the back of the spoon, 2 to 3 minutes. Pour the custard through the strainer into the prepared bowl and stir until cool. Remove the bowl from the ice bath, cover, and refrigerate the custard until cold, at least 4 hours or up to overnight.

Whisk the custard to recombine. Freeze and churn in an ice cream maker according to the manufacturer's instructions. Once the ice cream has finished churning, mix in the praline pieces. For a soft consistency, serve the ice cream right away; for a firmer consistency, transfer it to a container, cover, and allow to harden in the freezer for 2 to 3 hours.

NOTE You'll need a candy thermometer to test the temperature of the sugar mixture when making the pralines.

SPICY
AND BOOZY
FLAVORS

SABORES PICOSITOS Y BORRACHITOS

This chapter has an assortment of ice creams and sorbets that are spicy, boozy, or a bit of both. Although each of these recipes could have been put into other chapters, I thought it would be good to have them all in one section.

In Mexico, the flavors of the snacks and junk candy that I grew up with have many layers—sweet, salty, spicy, acidic. We love mixtures of flavors, especially if they are tangy and have a bit of chile. We snack on mangoes and cucumbers tossed with salt, lime, and chile. Popcorn in many movie theaters is tossed in a chile-salt mixture, and potato chips are often doused with a concoction of sauces—Maggi Seasoning (a wheat-based product similar to soy sauce), Worcestershire sauce, some kind of hot sauce, and fresh lime juice. My favorite candy growing up was *rielitos*, a brown candy made of *tejocate*, a slightly sour fruit that looks like a small crabapple. The candy is like a thick fruit leather but a bit drier, and it is spicy, a little sweet, and a little salty. It may not sound that appealing, but we go crazy for these kinds of flavors!

The thing to know about chile is that it isn't about being too spicy and overpowering the other flavors. It's about the balance of all the flavors together, with a punch that complements or heightens everything else. You will find many stands that have no chile in the sorbets or ice creams but instead have

cups ready filled with some sort of chile or *chamoy* (pickled plum sauce, see page 12), as they go with so many different flavors—particularly most, if not all, *nieves*. The ice cream is scooped or placed inside with a paddle, and you can get extra chile to top as well. There are also frozen treats, including *mangonadas*, *chamoyadas*, and *diablitos*, that may vary slightly depending on where you are, but all include some kind of fruit-based frozen treat, sauce, chile, and salt. Mexicans love them!

liquor flavored with rum, but many ice cream makers also use specific liquors from their region, such as mezcal in Oaxaca. There is actually a Star Wars–inspired ice cream shop in Mexico City that opened a few years ago with the brilliant name of Helado Obscuro, which translates to "obscure ice cream" or "dark ice cream." They make only boozy flavors and are very playful with their names and inspirations, such as Pink Pony, made with strawberries, pink peppercorns, and berry liqueur; and Alice in Wonderbra, which is made with chocolate, bourbon, and hazelnuts. To me, this place is an example of a business that focuses primarily on the concept and branding (which are brilliant) more than the quality, but it is fun and very popular, for good reason.

You can always increase the alcohol in the boozy recipes, but note that the more alcohol an ice cream has, the less likely it is to freeze. You may get a texture that is closer to soft-serve or a slushie, and that's not necessarily a bad thing, depending on what you want (see Rum Raisin Ice Cream, page 128).

As far as boozy—or *borrachito*—flavors, some great spirits and liquors are made in Mexico, including tequila, Kahlúa, mezcal, *tepache* (fermented pineapple drink), *pulque* (fermented agave drink), beer, and many others, so it's only natural that they would creep into ice creams. Plus, Mexican culture is colorful and playful, and that is reflected in a lot of our food as well.

There are some common boozy flavors, like rum raisin, some kind of margarita, and *rompope*, a sweet, custard-based

MOLE ICE CREAM

The term *mole,* derived from the Nahuatl (Aztec) word *mulli,* describes a type of sauce. There are a lot of different kinds of moles, as each region in Mexico has its specialty and each family has a recipe that's handed down from generation to generation. Mole bases can be powders or pastes, and are made with chiles, nuts, seeds, dried fruits, and sometimes chocolate, all ground together. The process of making mole requires multiple steps, and since there are so many ingredients, the process can take days.

Although mole is most commonly used in savory dishes, I've tried mole ice cream several times, but none tasted quite how I wanted it to. After lots of testing, I finally achieved the mole ice cream that I was after: sweet, spicy, nutty, complex, layered, and balanced.

The mole paste takes quite a bit of time and effort to make, but you can make it ahead and keep it in the freezer for up to four months. You'll have enough mole paste for several batches of ice cream.

MAKES ABOUT
· 1½ ·
QUARTS

MOLE PASTE

1 small (3-ounce) tomato

3 ounces tomatillos, husked and rinsed

12 ancho chiles

12 guajillo chiles

6 pasilla chiles

6 morita chiles

½ cup plus 1 tablespoon sunflower or canola oil, plus more as needed

½ cup whole almonds

½ cup pecans

⅓ cup dark raisins

To make the mole paste, adjust an oven rack to the uppermost position and preheat the broiler. Line a small baking sheet with aluminum foil.

Using a paring knife, core the tomato and cut a small X on the bottom. Place the tomato and tomatillos on the prepared baking sheet and broil until charred on all sides, 10 to 12 minutes. Remove from the oven and allow to cool. Once cool enough to handle, peel the tomato and tomatillos and set aside.

Wipe all of the chiles with a cloth. Using a paring knife, slit each chile lengthwise and remove the seeds, stems, and veins; reserve the seeds if you prefer a mole with some spiciness. In a heavy-bottomed medium skillet, warm the ½ cup of oil over medium heat until shimmering. Working in batches and with one variety at a time, fry the chiles in the oil, turning them with tongs, until puffed and slightly darker

1 ripe plantain, peeled and sliced

⅓ cup pumpkin seeds

1 (3-inch) piece Mexican cinnamon

¼ teaspoon ground allspice

⅛ teaspoon ground black pepper

6 ounces good-quality Mexican chocolate, chopped

5 ounces piloncillo (see page 16), chopped, or ⅔ cup packed dark brown sugar

1 teaspoon salt

3 cups whole milk

¾ cup sugar

½ teaspoon kosher salt

1 (5-inch) piece Mexican cinnamon, broken into bits

6 large egg yolks

3 tablespoons cornstarch

Toasted nuts or seeds, for garnish

in color, about 1 minute per side. As the chiles are done, transfer them to a large heatproof bowl. When all of the chiles are fried, add enough water to cover and allow to soften for 30 minutes. Drain the chiles.

In the same oil used to fry the chiles, fry the almonds and pecans over medium heat, stirring occasionally, until golden, about 5 minutes. Transfer to a large bowl. If needed, add more oil to the skillet and fry the raisins, stirring occasionally, until plumped, about 3 minutes, then transfer to the bowl with the nuts. If needed, add more oil to the skillet and fry the plantain slices until golden brown, about 5 minutes, then transfer to the bowl.

In a small skillet, toast the chile seeds (if using) over medium heat until fragrant, about 1 minute, then transfer to a small bowl. In the same skillet, toast the pumpkin seeds over medium heat until lightly golden, about 2 minutes, then transfer to the bowl with the chile seeds. Finally, toast the cinnamon over medium heat until fragrant, 2 to 3 minutes, then transfer to the bowl.

In a blender or food processor, combine the tomato and tomatillos, the drained chiles, the nut mixture, the seed mixture, the allspice, and the black pepper. Puree until a uniformly smooth paste forms, scraping down the sides as needed, 6 to 8 minutes. If necessary, add up to ¾ cup water to help the mixture blend.

In a large saucepan, warm 1 tablespoon of oil over medium heat until shimmering. Add the paste and cook, stirring occasionally, until it bubbles and sputters (cover with a splatter screen if you have one). Add the chocolate and piloncillo and continue to cook, stirring, until the chocolate has melted and the piloncillo has dissolved, about 10 minutes. Stir in the salt. Transfer to a heatproof bowl and allow to cool. Cover and refrigerate until ready to use.

. . . CONTINUED

In a saucepan, combine the milk, sugar, salt, and cinnamon. Bring to a simmer over medium heat, stirring to dissolve the sugar. Pour the mixture through a fine-mesh strainer set over a heatproof bowl. Return the milk to the saucepan and warm over medium heat. Meanwhile, partially fill a large bowl with ice and water, place a medium bowl in the ice water, and set a fine-mesh strainer across the top.

In a heatproof bowl, whisk together the eggs yolks and cornstarch. Gradually ladle about half of the hot milk into the egg mixture while whisking continuously. Return this mixture to the pan and cook, stirring continuously, until the custard reaches a simmer and is thick enough to coat the back of the spoon. Pour the custard through the strainer into the prepared bowl.

Add 1¼ cups of mole paste to the bowl and whisk until well blended and cool. Remove the bowl from the ice bath, cover, and refrigerate until the custard is cold, at least 2 hours or up to overnight.

Freeze and churn in an ice cream maker according to the manufacturer's instructions. For a soft consistency, serve the ice cream right away; for a firmer consistency, transfer it to a container, cover, and allow to harden in the freezer for 2 to 3 hours. Serve sprinkled with toasted nuts or seeds.

NOTE I have a mild allergy to sesame seeds and peanuts, so I didn't use either in this recipe. However, if you'd like to include them, toast ½ cup sesame seeds after toasting the pumpkin seeds. Add the sesame seeds and ⅓ cup toasted peanuts to the food processor when grinding the paste.

SPICY WATERMELON SORBET

NIEVE DE SANDÍA PICOSITA

In Mexico, a very popular street snack is cut-up fresh fruit sprinkled with salt, ground chiles, and lime juice. Watermelon, mango, orange, and pineapple are the most common. Cucumber and jicama are served this way too. Fruit sorbets are often flavored with the same seasonings, but this refreshing watermelon sorbet uses fresh green chiles, not ground chiles, for spiciness.

I like this sorbet with the melon seeds mixed in, as seeing them in there makes me feel as though I'm taking bites of the fresh fruit. But it's surprising to me that it's so difficult to find watermelons with seeds in the United States. You can use seedless watermelon, of course—the sorbet will still taste amazing.

MAKES ABOUT

· 1½ ·

QUARTS

6 cups cubed watermelon (about 2 pounds; see Note)

¾ cup sugar

3 tablespoons light corn syrup

Juice of 2 limes

2 serrano chiles, or 1 small jalapeño chile, coarsely chopped, with seeds

1 teaspoon salt

Pinch of ground piquín chile, plus more to taste (optional)

Salted ground chiles, for sprinkling (optional, look for Tajín brand)

In a blender, combine the watermelon, sugar, corn syrup, lime juice, chopped chiles, salt, and piquín chile. Puree until smooth. Taste and, if desired, add more piquín chile. Pour into a container, cover, and refrigerate until cold, at least 2 hours or up to overnight.

Freeze and churn in an ice cream maker according to the manufacturer's instructions. When the sorbet has finished churning, mix in the reserved watermelon seeds (if using). For a soft consistency, serve the sorbet right away; for a firmer consistency, transfer it to a container, cover, and allow to harden in the freezer for 2 to 3 hours. Serve sprinkled with salted ground chiles, if desired.

NOTE If you are using watermelon with seeds and would like to add the seeds to the sorbet, remove the seeds before cutting the melon into cubes, and then mix them in after churning the sorbet. If the seeds are simply left in the flesh, they will break down when the melon is pureed.

CHOCOLATE-CHILE ICE CREAM

HELADO DE CHOCOLATE CON CHILE

At La Newyorkina, customers sometimes ask how spicy our Mexican chocolate ice cream is, and to be honest, it drives me a little crazy because traditional Mexican chocolate does *not* contain chile. I did, however, want to develop a chocolate-chile ice cream for this book because the combination dates back a long time and *is* awesome!

I use two different varieties of dried chiles here: chipotle chiles for their smokiness, mild sweetness, and moderate spiciness and ancho chiles, which have prunelike notes and almost no heat at all (pasilla chiles are a good alternative to anchos). If you have your own favorite types of dried chiles, feel free to use them. Unlike most chocolate ice creams, this one isn't custard based; it's thickened with cornstarch, but you'll be surprised how rich and chocolaty it tastes. The touch of espresso really rounds out the chile and chocolate flavors.

MAKES ABOUT

· 1 ·

QUART

6 chipotle chiles

2 ancho chiles

6 ounces good-quality bittersweet chocolate, coarsely chopped

3 tablespoons cornstarch

3 cups half-and-half

2/3 cup unsweetened Dutch-process cocoa powder

1 cup sugar

1 teaspoon instant espresso powder

1 teaspoon salt

Wipe all of the chiles with a cloth. Remove and discard the stems from all of the chiles, and remove and discard the seeds from the ancho chiles. In a heavy-bottomed skillet over medium heat, toast the chiles, pressing them flat against the surface of the pan, until fragrant, about 10 seconds per side. Put the chiles in a bowl, add very hot (not boiling) water to cover, and allow to soak until softened, about 30 minutes. Drain, reserving the soaking liquid. In a blender or mini food processor, puree the chiles until they form a thick paste, adding 2 to 3 tablespoons of the reserved soaking water as needed. Set the chile paste aside.

Put the chocolate in a large heatproof bowl and place a fine-mesh strainer over the top. In a small bowl, whisk together the cornstarch and 1/2 cup of the half-and-half. In a saucepan, combine the remaining 2 1/2 cups of half-and-half and the cocoa powder, sugar, espresso, and salt. Bring to a simmer over medium heat, stirring to dissolve the sugar. Whisk the cornstarch mixture to recombine, then add it to the half-and-half in the saucepan and cook, stirring continuously, until the mixture returns to a simmer and is smooth and thickened, 3 to 5 minutes. Pour the mixture through the fine-mesh strainer onto the chocolate. Allow to stand for 1 to 2 minutes to melt the chocolate, then whisk until smooth and incorporated. Whisk in 2 tablespoons of the chile paste and taste. If desired, add more chile paste, keeping in mind that once frozen, the ice cream will taste a little less spicy (leftover chile paste can be refrigerated for up to 3 days or frozen for up to 1 month). Allow to cool. Cover and refrigerate until cold, at least 4 hours or up to overnight.

Freeze and churn in an ice cream maker according to the manufacturer's instructions. For a soft consistency, serve the ice cream right away; for a firmer consistency, transfer it to a container, cover, and allow to harden in the freezer for 2 to 3 hours.

NOTE Be sure to use dry chipotle chiles here, not the chipotles in adobo sauce that are sold in a can.

RUM RAISIN ICE CREAM

HELADO DE RON CON PASAS

This is a very popular flavor in Mexico. Many versions of this ice cream are custard based, but my version is thickened with a bit of cornstarch, as many Mexican ice creams are. I also include some *crema*, or Mexican sour cream—I love the acidic notes of the *crema* paired with the sweetness of the raisins. Because this ice cream contains a lot of rum, it doesn't freeze solid, but that's kind of the point. I like to eat it straight out of the machine—it's like a super-thick, really tasty milkshake for adults!

MAKES ABOUT
· 1 ·
QUART

1 cup raisins
1 cup dark rum
2 cups whole milk
1 tablespoon cornstarch
1 cup heavy cream
¾ cup sugar
1 teaspoon kosher salt
⅓ cup crema
or sour cream
½ teaspoon ground
Mexican cinnamon
(optional)

In a small bowl, mix together the raisins and rum. Cover and let soak at room temperature until the raisins are plump, at least 6 hours or up to overnight.

In a second small bowl, whisk together ½ cup of the milk and the cornstarch. In a saucepan, combine the remaining 1½ cups of milk and the cream, sugar, and salt. Bring to a simmer over medium heat, stirring to dissolve the sugar. Whisk the cornstarch mixture to recombine, then add it to the milk mixture in the saucepan and cook, stirring continuously, until the mixture returns to a simmer and has thickened slightly. Remove from the heat and whisk in the crema and cinnamon. Pour the mixture through a fine-mesh strainer set over a bowl. Let cool. Cover and refrigerate until cold, at least 4 hours or up to overnight.

Freeze and churn in an ice cream maker according to the manufacturer's instructions. When the ice cream has finished churning, mix in the raisins and rum. For a soft consistency, serve the ice cream right away; for a firmer consistency, transfer it to a container, cover, and allow to harden in the freezer for at least 4 hours.

CARAMELIZED FIG ICE CREAM WITH MEZCAL AND QUESO FRESCO

NIEVE DE QUESO CON MEZCAL E HIGOS CARAMELIZADOS

In Oaxaca, if you look hard enough you can find a wonderful ice cream made with figs and mezcal. Sometimes the figs are dried, but most often they are fresh. Mezcal, a spirit made with roasted agave, has a distinct smokiness that goes beautifully with ripe figs.

In this version, the figs are cooked with butter and brown sugar until caramelized, and a bit of *queso fresco* adds a slightly salty, savory edge that complements the figs perfectly. I really wanted the mezcal flavor to come through, so I put a bit in both the figs and the ice cream. With caramelly, smoky, salty, and boozy flavors, this is an ice cream you definitely don't want to miss!

MAKES ABOUT
· 1¼ ·
QUARTS

2 tablespoons
unsalted butter

½ cup packed
dark brown sugar

1 pound fresh
Mission figs, halved

2 tablespoons water

6 tablespoons mezcal

½ teaspoon salt

3 tablespoons
cornstarch

3 cups whole milk

1 cup granulated sugar

4 ounces queso fresco
(see page 16)

In a large saucepan, melt the butter over medium heat. Add the brown sugar and stir to combine. Add the figs and water and cook, stirring frequently, until the figs soften and the mixture looks a bit jamlike, 5 to 7 minutes. Remove from the heat, stir in 3 tablespoons of the mezcal and the salt, and allow to cool. Transfer to a container and refrigerate until ready to use, or for up to 2 days.

Partially fill a large bowl with ice and water, place a medium bowl in the ice water, and set a fine-mesh strainer across the top.

In a small bowl, whisk together the cornstarch and ½ cup of the milk. In a saucepan, combine the remaining 2½ cups of milk and the granulated sugar. Bring to a simmer over medium heat, stirring to dissolve the sugar. Whisk the cornstarch mixture to recombine and then add it to the milk in the saucepan. Cook, stirring continuously,

until the mixture returns to a simmer and has thickened. Pour the mixture through the strainer into the prepared bowl. Add the queso fresco and the remaining 3 tablespoons of mezcal and stir until cool. Cover and refrigerate until cold, at least 4 hours or up to overnight.

Freeze and churn in an ice cream maker according to the manufacturer's instructions. Transfer the ice cream to a container, cover, and allow to harden in the freezer for 2 to 3 hours.

NOTE Avoid gimmicky mezcal with a worm inside the bottle because the alcohol is of poor quality.

CUCUMBER-LIME SORBET WITH SERRANO CHILE

NIEVE DE PEPINO CON
CHILE SERRANO Y LIMÓN

MAKES ABOUT
· 1½ ·
QUARTS

2 cups water

1 cup sugar

3 tablespoons
light corn syrup

2 serrano or
jalapeño chiles,
stemmed and seeded

1 teaspoon kosher salt

2 pounds cucumbers,
peeled, seeded, and cut
into large chunks

⅔ cup freshly squeezed
lime juice

Cucumber-lime is one of our most popular *paleta* flavors at
La Newyorkina. It's extremely refreshing, and I always sprinkle
lots of salted chile on top. For this book, I wanted to develop a
sorbet with that ingredient combination but with a bit of spice to
the sorbet itself. Serrano chiles are just the thing: they have good
heat and a very bright, crisp flavor that pairs perfectly with
cucumber and lime. If you can't find serrano chiles, you can use
jalapeños instead.

In a small saucepan, combine 1 cup of the water and the sugar. Bring
to a simmer over medium heat, stirring to dissolve the sugar. Remove
from the heat, stir in the corn syrup, and allow to cool.

In a blender, combine the remaining 1 cup of water, the chiles, and
the salt and puree until there are no visible chunks. Pour the mixture
through a fine-mesh strainer set over a bowl. Return the strained chile
water to the blender, add the cucumbers, and blend until smooth.
Pour the mixture through the fine-mesh strainer set over the bowl.
Stir in the lime juice and the sugar syrup. Cover and refrigerate until
cold, at least 4 hours or up to 8 hours.

Freeze and churn in an ice cream maker according to the manufacturer's
instructions. For a soft consistency, serve the sorbet right away; for a
firmer consistency, transfer it to a container, cover, and allow to harden
in the freezer for 2 to 3 hours.

NOTE I like to slice a couple of serrano chiles into very thin rounds, toss them in a bit
of sugar, and serve them on top of this sorbet as a garnish.

SPICY AND BOOZY FLAVORS

TROPICAL MARGARITA SORBET

NIEVE DE MARGARITA TROPICAL

When I was developing a margarita sorbet for La Newyorkina, I wanted flavors that were more interesting and exciting than the usual citrus. I love the combination of mango and passion fruit—they strike a perfect sweet-tart balance—so I created this *nieve de margarita tropical* with those fruits as the stars. It quickly became one our best sellers!

You can use whatever kind of tequila you like, but I think the mild flavor of *blanco* (white) lets the fruit flavors really shine.

MAKES ABOUT
· 1¼ ·
QUARTS

1 cup sugar

1 cup passion fruit puree

1½ pounds ripe mangoes, peeled, pitted, and cubed

Grated zest of 2 limes

3 tablespoons blanco (white) tequila

1 tablespoon orange liqueur

1 tablespoon light corn syrup

½ teaspoon kosher salt

In a small saucepan, combine the sugar and passion fruit puree. Bring to a simmer over medium heat, stirring to dissolve the sugar. Remove from the heat and allow to cool.

In a blender, combine the passion fruit mixture, cubed mango, lime zest, tequila, orange liqueur, corn syrup, and salt. Puree until smooth. Pour the mixture into a bowl, cover, and refrigerate until cold, at least 4 hours or up to overnight.

Freeze and churn in an ice cream maker according to the manufacturer's instructions. For a soft consistency (the best, in my opinion), serve the sorbet right away; for a firmer consistency, transfer it to a container, cover, and allow to harden in the freezer for 2 to 3 hours.

MEXICAN ICE CREAM

SOUR CREAM ICE CREAM WITH CHILE AND APRICOTS

Last year, I picked up some incredibly plump apricots that were sweet but a little tangy. When I got to the kitchen, I cut up an apricot and sprinkled on some chile and salt to eat as a snack. At the same time, a batch of sour cream *paletas* was coming out of the freezer and I took a bite. The combination was so incredible, my head started to spin! So I tossed some apricots with guajillo chiles (mild chiles with fruity notes) and *piloncillo* (Mexican unrefined sugar) and roasted them to concentrate their flavor. I scrapped the idea of putting the apricots into *paletas* and instead came up with this *crema*-based ice cream.

MAKES ABOUT
· 1 ·
QUART

8 guajillo chiles

6 large apricots
(about 1½ pounds),
pitted and quartered

2 ounces piloncillo
(see page 16), chopped,
or ¼ cup packed
dark brown sugar

1 vanilla bean,
split lengthwise

¼ cup water

1 tablespoon honey

¾ teaspoon kosher salt

2 cups Mexican crema
or sour cream

⅔ cup sugar

1 tablespoon plus
1 teaspoon cornstarch

1 cup whole milk

Wipe the chiles with a cloth. Cut off the stems and remove the seeds and veins. Put the chiles in a bowl, add hot (not boiling) water to cover, and let soak until softened, about 5 minutes. Drain the chiles and cut into thin strips.

Preheat the oven to 400°F.

In a shallow baking dish just large enough to hold the apricots in a single layer, gently toss the apricots and piloncillo. Using a paring knife, scrape the seeds from the vanilla bean halves into the apricots, and then drop in the pods. Toss again, then arrange the apricots in a single layer. Scatter 2 tablespoons of the guajillo chiles over the top, pour in the water, drizzle with the honey, and sprinkle in ½ teaspoon of the salt. Roast the apricots, occasionally basting with the syrup in the dish, until tender and jamlike, about 15 minutes. Allow to cool, drain off the juices, and transfer the apricots to a container. Cover and refrigerate until ready to use, or for up to 2 weeks. Drain before using.

. . . CONTINUED

SPICY AND BOOZY FLAVORS

Partially fill a large bowl with ice water. In a medium bowl, stir together the remaining guajillo chiles and the crema. Place the bowl in the ice water and set a fine-mesh strainer over the bowl.

In a small saucepan, combine the sugar, the cornstarch, and the remaining ¼ teaspoon of salt. Whisk in about half of the milk until well combined, then whisk in the remaining milk. Cook over medium heat until the mixture is warm and foamy, stirring continuously. Lower the heat and continue to whisk until the mixture thickens, loses the foam, and begins to boil. Pour the mixture through the strainer into the crema. Whisk until well combined and cool. Cover and refrigerate until cold, at least 3 hours or up to overnight.

Freeze and churn in an ice cream maker according to the manufacturer's instructions. When the ice cream has finished churning, mix in the apricots. For a soft consistency, serve the ice cream right away; for a firmer consistency, transfer it to a container, cover, and allow to harden in the freezer for 2 to 3 hours.

MEXICAN ICE CREAM

HIBISCUS-SANGRIA SORBET

NIEVE DE SANGRIA CON JAMAICA

At La Newyorkina, we make a hibiscus-sangria *paleta*, but I thought the flavors and textures would be even better as a sorbet. To achieve deep flavor, I like to use a medium-bodied red wine with fruity notes that's not too sweet, such as a Merlot. The sorbet itself is moderately sweet, but the hibiscus adds that acidity and tartness that Mexicans love. The chunks of fruit add lots of texture to this elegant, burgundy-colored *nieve*.

MAKES ABOUT
· 1¼ ·
QUARTS

2 cups red wine

1 cup water

1½ cups dried hibiscus flowers (see page 13)

2 tablespoons light corn syrup

1 cup sugar

Grated zest and juice of 1 small orange

1 small peach

1 small tart apple (such as Crispin or Granny Smith)

½ cup red grapes

½ cup strawberries

In a saucepan, combine the wine, water, hibiscus, corn syrup, and ¾ cup of the sugar. Bring to a simmer over medium heat and cook for 5 minutes, stirring to dissolve the sugar. Remove from the heat, stir in the orange zest and juice, and allow to cool to room temperature. Pour the mixture through a fine-mesh strainer set over a bowl. Cover and refrigerate until cold, at least 3 hours or up to overnight.

About 15 minutes before you are ready to freeze the sorbet, pit and finely dice the peach. Core and finely dice the apple. Cut the grapes in half. Hull and finely dice the strawberries. Combine all of the fruit in a bowl, add the remaining ¼ cup of sugar, and toss to combine. Set aside.

Freeze and churn the hibiscus mixture in an ice cream maker according to the manufacturer's instructions. When the sorbet has finished churning, drain the fruit mixture in a fine-mesh strainer, then mix the fruit into the sorbet. Transfer to a container, cover, and allow to harden in the freezer for 2 to 3 hours.

MEXICAN "EGGNOG" ICE CREAM

HELADO DE ROMPOPE

Rompope is an eggnog-like, custard-based beverage flavored with rum, vanilla, and/or Mexican cinnamon, though more modern variations may include ingredients like pine nuts, coffee, and chocolate. *Rompope* is offered year-round, served over ice, and it's great made into gelatins, *paletas*, and, of course, ice cream.

MAKES ABOUT
· 1 ·
QUART

ROMPOPE
4 cups whole milk
1 cup sugar
Pinch of baking soda
1 (3-inch) piece
Mexican cinnamon
8 large egg yolks
½ cup dark rum or brandy
1 teaspoon
pure vanilla extract

2 cups half-and-half
⅔ cup sugar
1 teaspoon kosher salt
1 teaspoon pure
vanilla extract
(preferably Mexican)

NOTE This ice cream is delicious plain, but if you want to add texture, mix in some chopped toasted pecans or almonds right after churning.

To make the rompope, combine the milk, sugar, baking soda, and cinnamon in a large saucepan and bring to a boil over medium-high heat, stirring to dissolve the sugar. Turn down the heat to maintain a steady simmer and cook for 30 minutes, or until the mixture reduces to about 3 cups.

In a heatproof bowl, whisk the egg yolks and gradually ladle in about 1 cup of the hot milk mixture while whisking continuously. Pour this mixture into the saucepan and cook over low heat, stirring continuously, until slightly thickened, 5 to 7 minutes. Immediately pour the mixture into a bowl set in an ice bath and allow to cool to room temperature. Remove and discard the cinnamon and stir in the rum and vanilla. Cover and refrigerate until cold.

In a small saucepan, combine 1 cup of the half-and-half and the sugar. Bring to a simmer over medium heat, stirring to dissolve the sugar. Add the remaining half-and-half, then pour the mixture into a bowl and allow to cool to room temperature. Stir in the salt, vanilla, and 1 cup of the chilled rompope (reserve the rest for drinking). Cover and refrigerate until cold, at least 2 hours or up to overnight.

Freeze and churn in an ice cream maker according to the manufacturer's instructions. Transfer to a container, cover, and allow to harden in the freezer for 2 to 3 hours.

DEVILED MANGO SORBET

NIEVE DE MANGO ENDIABLADO

In Mexico, the combination of mango and chile is common in candies and snacks, but this silky smooth sorbet is hands down one of the very best ways to enjoy those flavors together. The sweet-tart quality of the mango, the spiciness of the chile, and a distinct saltiness make it downright irresistible!

Neverías typically serve this sorbet in a cup with some kind of chile sauce and ground chiles. My favorite way is to serve it with *chamoy* (pickled plum sauce) and Miguelito brand seasoning, but really, as long as there is some type of ground chile and salt, you can't go wrong.

MAKES ABOUT
· 1 ·
QUART

⅓ cup water

1 cup sugar

3 piquín chiles

2½ pounds
ripe mangoes, peeled,
pitted, and diced
(about 5¾ cups)

Juice of 1 lime

¾ teaspoon kosher salt

1 teaspoon ground
piquín chile or
cayenne pepper,
plus more to taste

In a small saucepan, combine the water and sugar. Bring to a simmer over medium heat, stirring to dissolve the sugar. Remove from the heat, stir in the whole chiles, and allow to cool for 1 hour.

Remove and discard the chiles from the sugar syrup. In a blender, combine the sugar syrup and diced mangoes and puree until smooth. Add the lime juice, salt, and ground chile and blend to combine. Taste the puree and, if desired, mix in additional ground chile, keeping in mind that once frozen, the sorbet will taste a little less spicy. Pour the mixture through a fine-mesh strainer set over a bowl. Cover and refrigerate until cold, at least 4 hours or up to overnight.

Freeze and churn in an ice cream maker according to the manufacturer's instructions. For a soft consistency, serve the sorbet right away; for a firmer consistency, transfer it to a container, cover, and allow to harden in the freezer for 2 to 3 hours.

SPICY TAMARIND "PULPARINDO" CANDY SORBET

NIEVE DE PULPARINDO CON CHILE

MAKES ABOUT
• 1¼ •
QUARTS

One of my best friends, Josefina Santacruz, is an amazing Mexican chef. She often talks about the umami flavor that Mexicans love. It's that sour-salty-sweet that you experience on the tip of your tongue, and it makes us salivate just thinking about it.

When I tried this flavor, I thought of Josefina immediately and knew I needed to include it in the book! Tamarind sorbet is one of the most popular (and my personal favorite) *nieve*, but this is a modern version that has become very popular in Guadalajara. No doubt it will quickly spread through the rest of Mexico.

8 ounces tamarind pods (see page 16)

4 cups water, plus more if needed

1 cup sugar

1 teaspoon kosher salt

1 to 3 teaspoons ground piquín or árbol chile, plus more for serving if desired

6 ounces soft tamarind candy, such as Pulparindo, torn into chunks

Chamoy (see page 12; optional), to pour on top

Peel off the shell of the tamarind pods and discard them, along with any stringy bits. Put the tamarind pulp and the water in a medium saucepan over medium heat and bring to a boil. Turn down the heat and simmer, stirring from time to time, until the tamarind is tender, about 30 minutes. Allow to cool.

Strain the mixture through a fine-mesh strainer set over a bowl, saving both the pulp and the liquid. Measure the liquid, adding more water to make 3½ cups. Return the liquid to the saucepan, add the sugar, and cook, stirring continuously, until the sugar dissolves.

Press the tamarind pulp through the strainer (using your hands will be messy but it's the best way) and add to the saucepan. Stir in the salt and 1 teaspoon of the chile, tasting and adding more until the mixture has enough heat, keeping in mind that the spiciness will diminish slightly once the sorbet is frozen. Cover and refrigerate until cold for at least 4 hours or up to overnight.

Freeze and churn in an ice cream maker according to the manufacturer's instructions. Once it has partially frozen, add the candy, then continue processing until frozen. Transfer to a container, cover, and allow to harden in the freezer for 2 to 3 hours. Serve topped with chamoy if desired.

NOTE You can find tamarind candy at many bodegas, Latin groceries, and online.

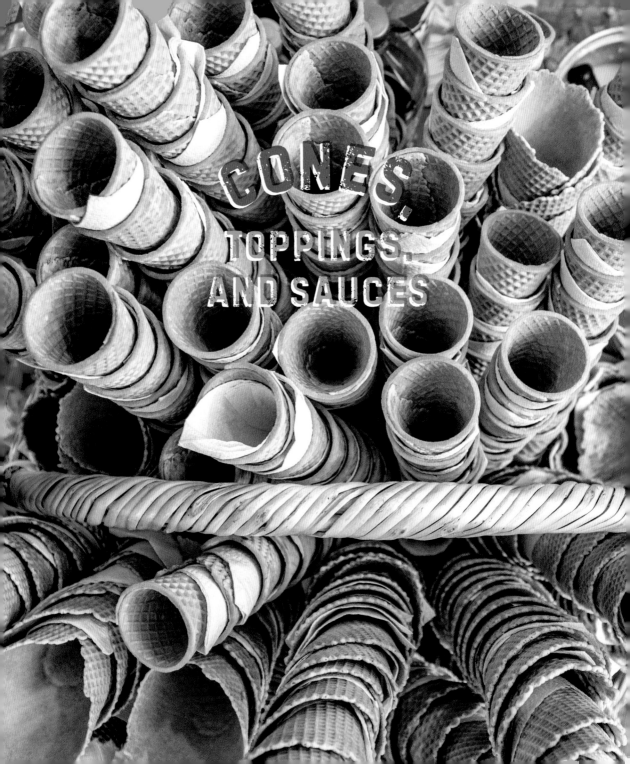

CONES,
TOPPINGS,
AND SAUCES

CHERRY-HIBISCUS COMPOTE

COMPOTA DE CEREZAS CON JAMAICA

MAKES ABOUT
· 5 ·
CUPS

2 pounds fresh or frozen
Bing cherries, pitted
(about 4½ cups)

¾ cup sugar

½ cup water

¾ cup dried
hibiscus flowers
(see page 13)

Big pinch of kosher salt

I love cherries. Every summer, I fully expect to experience many bellyaches because I can't stop—I'll eat a whole bag of cherries in one sitting!

This compote, with its stunning, deep red color, gets its sweetness from the cherries (and sugar, of course) and its tartness from the hibiscus flowers. You can serve it warm or at room temperature. I think it goes wonderfully with Horchata Ice Cream (page 93).

In a large heavy-bottomed saucepan, combine all of the ingredients. Bring to a boil over medium heat, then turn down the heat to maintain a simmer and cook, stirring occasionally, until the juices are thick enough to coat the back of the spoon, about 10 minutes. Remove from the heat and allow to cool. Stored in an airtight container in the refrigerator, the compote will keep for up to 1 week.

NOTE I prefer this compote made with Bing cherries, but any type of sweet cherry will work nicely.

PASSION FRUIT
CARAMEL SAUCE

CARAMELO DE MARACUYÁ

This is not your standard caramel sauce that's thick and enriched with heavy cream. Rather, it's slightly tangy from the passion fruit, with bittersweet notes from the caramelized sugar. Just a bit of butter smooths out the flavors and adds a touch of richness. This sauce is a perfect accompaniment to Rice Pudding Ice Cream (page 75).

MAKES ABOUT
· 3 ·
CUPS

2 cups sugar

½ cup water

2 teaspoons
light corn syrup

1⅓ cups passion fruit
puree

4 tablespoons unsalted
butter, cut into pieces

½ teaspoon kosher salt

In a large heavy-bottomed saucepan, combine the sugar, water, and corn syrup. Bring to a simmer over medium heat, stirring to dissolve the sugar and occasionally brushing down the sides of pan with a wet pastry brush to wash off any sugar crystals. Increase the heat to medium-high and allow to boil without stirring until the syrup is dark amber in color, about 8 minutes. Remove the pan from the heat. Carefully add the passion fruit puree (it will bubble and splatter, so be careful as you pour it in), butter, and salt and whisk to incorporate as much as possible (the caramel will harden a bit). Set the pan over medium-low heat, bring to a simmer, and cook, stirring, until the caramel has dissolved and the sauce is smooth. Remove from the heat and allow to cool. Stored in an airtight container in the refrigerator, the sauce will keep for up to 10 days. Serve the sauce warm or at room temperature.

NOTE Frozen passion fruit puree is sold in many Latin American markets and specialty grocery stores.

GOAT'S MILK CARAMEL

CAJETA

I have such a weakness for *cajeta*. I absolutely love its milky, ever-so-slightly-tangy, subtle caramel flavor. As a kid, I used to sneak into the kitchen in the middle of the night and eat spoonfuls straight out of the jar. The sticky mess I left behind always gave me away in the morning, but thankfully my parents were amused rather than upset.

In Mexico, *cajeta* can be plain or flavored with liquors, vanilla, or cinnamon; the consistency can be dense and spreadable or thin and saucelike. The best *cajeta* is made in Celaya, in the state of Guanajuato. There you can even find it packed in oval wooden containers with the surface of the *cajeta* richly caramelized—this type is meant to be eaten with a spoon. My recipe makes *cajeta* that is thick and sticky but pourable, so you can drizzle it onto ice cream or pancakes—or eat it from a spoon if you like.

MAKES ABOUT

· 1 ·

CUP

4 cups goat's milk or a combination of cow's and goat's milks, preferably unpasteurized

1¼ cups sugar

¼ teaspoon baking soda

½ teaspoon pure vanilla extract

Pinch of kosher salt

NOTE Unpasteurized goat's milk makes the very best *cajeta*, but pasteurized goat's milk works well too.

In a large heavy-bottomed saucepan, stir together the milk, sugar, and baking soda. Bring to a boil over high heat, then turn down the heat to maintain a brisk simmer and cook, stirring occasionally, until the mixture has thickened and is dark caramel in color, 1 to 1½ hours; stir more frequently as the mixture becomes thicker. Transfer to a heatproof bowl and allow to cool. Stir in the vanilla and salt. Stored in an airtight container in the refrigerator, the caramel will keep for up to 10 days.

MEXICAN HOT FUDGE

HOT FUDGE À LA MEXICANA

There is a store in Mexico City called Sanborns. It is a very peculiar place: it sells electronics, books, pharmacy items, and other random things, and inside the store is a restaurant that serves, for the most part, home-style Mexican food. But this is where, as a child, I had my very first American ice cream sundae! And with a Sanborns sundae is how my father would bribe me whenever he needed something. So although hot fudge is not a traditional Mexican ice cream topping, it's one of my favorites because it makes me nostalgic. To this day, if I'm feeling stressed and craving comfort food, a hot fudge sundae does the trick. My version of this sauce has the smooth, slightly chewy consistency of American hot fudge but the cinnamon-spiced flavor of Mexican chocolate.

MAKES ABOUT · 2 · CUPS

2/3 cup heavy cream

1/2 cup light corn syrup

1/4 cup packed dark brown sugar

1/4 cup unsweetened Dutch-process cocoa powder

1/2 teaspoon kosher salt

6 ounces good-quality Mexican chocolate, chopped

2 tablespoons unsalted butter

1 teaspoon pure vanilla extract

In a saucepan, combine the cream, corn syrup, brown sugar, cocoa powder, salt, and half of the chopped chocolate. Bring to a simmer over medium heat and cook, whisking continuously, until the chocolate is melted and the mixture is smooth. Turn down the heat to low and simmer gently, stirring occasionally, until the mixture thickens slightly, about 5 minutes. Add the butter and the remaining chopped chocolate and whisk until smooth. Remove from the heat, stir in the vanilla, and allow to cool. Stored in an airtight container in the refrigerator, the hot fudge will keep for up to 2 weeks. Serve the sauce warm.

CANDIED PUMPKIN SEEDS

PEPITAS GARAPIÑADAS

MAKES ABOUT
· 3 ·
CUPS

1 cup sugar

1 to 2 teaspoons ground piquín or árbol chile (optional)

1 teaspoon kosher salt

1 large egg white

3 cups pumpkin seeds

These candied *pepitas* are very quick and easy to make, and they add a delicious and unexpected texture to ice creams. I particularly love them with Chocolate-Chile Ice Cream (page 126) and Mole Ice Cream (page 120). The chile is optional, but I prefer these pumpkin seeds with a spicy kick.

Preheat the oven to 300°F. Lightly coat a rimmed baking sheet with a little vegetable oil or line it with parchment paper.

In a small bowl, mix together the sugar, chile (if using), and salt. In a medium bowl, beat the egg white with a fork until frothy. Add the pumpkin seeds and the sugar mixture and stir until the seeds are evenly coated. Spread the pumpkin seeds on the prepared baking sheet and bake, stirring a few times, until toasted, 10 to 12 minutes. Allow to cool to room temperature. Stored in an airtight container in a cool, dry spot, the pumpkin seeds will keep for up to 1 month.

VANILLA AND TEQUILA WHIPPED CREAM

CREMA BATIDA CON VAINILLA Y TEQUILA

MAKES ABOUT
· 2 ·
CUPS

1 cup cold heavy cream

2 tablespoons sugar

1 vanilla bean,
split lengthwise,
or 1 teaspoon
pure vanilla extract

1½ tablespoons
reposado or añejo tequila
(optional)

To me, perfect whipped cream should be slightly sweet and not overly aerated, which is why I always prefer making it by hand (I use a balloon whisk for best results). Your bowl and whisk should be chilled in advance so that the cream will whip more quickly.

Place a stainless steel bowl and a whisk in the freezer and allow to chill for 10 to 15 minutes.

In the chilled bowl, combine the cream and sugar. If using a vanilla bean, use a paring knife to scrape the seeds from the pod halves and add the seeds to the cream mixture (reserve the pods for another use; see page 69 for suggestions). With the chilled whisk, whip until the cream holds soft peaks when the whisk is lifted. Whisk in the tequila (and vanilla extract, if using). Continue whisking until the cream holds medium-stiff peaks. Use right away, or cover with plastic wrap and refrigerate for up to 2 days. (If refrigerated, whisk again for 10 to 15 seconds just before using.)

NOTE The tequila in this recipe is optional, and you can replace it with any liquor of your choice.

PILONCILLO CARAMELIZED PECANS

NUECES CARAMELIZADAS CON PILONCILLO

This recipe is so simple, but the flavor of the pecans is very deep and wonderfully complex, with rich molasses notes from the *piloncillo*. The look of the caramelized nuts is meant to be rustic, so don't worry about perfectly coating each pecan with sugar. The unevenness is part of the beauty, in my opinion.

Chopped up and stirred in after churning, these pecans add amazing texture and flavor to Nescafé Ice Cream (page 109) and Malt Ice Cream (page 104), but they would be delicious in so many others, too!

MAKES ABOUT
· 3 ·
CUPS

8 ounces piloncillo (see page 16), finely chopped

1 (1-inch) piece Mexican cinnamon

⅓ cup water

3¼ cups pecan halves

Lightly oil a rimmed baking sheet.

In a saucepan, combine the piloncillo, cinnamon, and water. Set the pan over medium heat and cook, stirring, until the piloncillo has dissolved and the mixture is bubbly, thick, and golden in color, 4 to 6 minutes. Add about one-third of the pecans and stir to coat. Add the remaining pecans in two more batches, stirring continuously. The piloncillo will begin to crystallize and look sandy. Continue stirring until all of the pecans are coated.

Pour the pecans onto the prepared baking sheet and separate them with a spoon. Remove the piece of cinnamon. Allow to cool to room temperature. Stored in an airtight container in a cool, dry spot, the pecans will keep for up to 3 weeks.

CONES, TOPPINGS, AND SAUCES

SPICY MANGOES

MANGUITOS ENCHILADOS

Xochimilco, in the center of Mexico, is famous for its candied fruits, such as figs, cherimoyas, papayas, and prickly pears. The fruits are first soaked in calcium oxide to create a shell on the outside of the fruit, and then put through a crystallization process that requires many steps and can take up to a week. This recipe is a simplified version of candied mangoes, but it still takes a few days to prepare. Fortunately, the fruits keep well, so I like to make a big batch if I'm going through the effort. This is a great topping for flavors like Lime Sorbet (page 29); Strawberry, Pineapple, and Orange Sorbet (page 45); and Tropical Margarita Sorbet (134).

MAKES ABOUT

▪ **3** ▪

CUPS

1 lime

1 pound ripe but firm mangoes

3 teaspoons kosher salt

3 cups sugar

2 cups water

¼ cup light corn syrup

⅓ cup ground guajillo, piquín, or árbol chiles, or a combination

Using a vegetable peeler, remove the lime zest in strips. Juice the lime.

Peel the mangoes and cut the flesh into large chunks or wedges. In a bowl, toss the mangoes with 1 teaspoon of the salt and the lime juice.

In a large saucepan, combine the sugar, water, corn syrup, and lime zest and bring to a boil over medium-high heat. Turn down the heat to medium-low, add the mango chunks, and simmer gently for 20 minutes, stirring occasionally. Remove from the heat, cover the pan with the lid or a piece of cheesecloth, and allow to stand overnight at room temperature.

The next day, uncover the pan, set it over medium heat, and bring the syrup to a simmer. Cook for 20 minutes, stirring occasionally and adjusting the heat as needed to maintain a simmer. Remove from the heat, cover with the lid or the cheesecloth, and allow to stand overnight at room temperature.

MEXICAN ICE CREAM

On the third day, once again uncover the pan, set it over medium heat, and bring to a simmer. Cook for only 5 minutes, stirring occasionally, then remove from the heat and allow to cool to room temperature. Once cool, use a slotted spoon to transfer the mango chunks to a wire rack set over a baking sheet. Discard the lime peel. Allow to drain until the mango pieces are no longer wet (they will be sticky), 8 to 10 hours.

In a bowl, stir together the ground chiles and the remaining 2 teaspoons of salt. Working in batches, toss the mango pieces in the chile mixture until coated on all sides. Stored in an airtight container in a cool, dry spot, the mangoes will keep for up to 1 month.

ACKNOWLEDGMENTS

This is such a hard part to write because there are so many people to thank and frankly they simply cannot all fit. I feel incredibly blessed and fortunate to be surrounded by so many caring and loving people.

First and foremost, I want to thank all of the ice cream makers, farmers, producers, and everyone who allowed me to share part of their stories and inspired me along the way. All of these people keep traditions alive and have so much pride and talent.

To my agent, Lisa Queen, for always having my back and pushing my ideas forward no matter how crazy they can be.

To Kelly, Betsy, Dawn, and everyone everyone at Ten Speed, for sharing so much passion and hard work with this beautiful book. For always allowing me to share my vision and heart, and for your incredible patience with me in the process.

Thank you Justin and Kaitlyn, for thinking outside the box and bringing so much to every aspect. And for being open to color!

Gracias Fernando, for capturing our Mexico with so much love, pride, and beauty, and for helping me tell the story.

To my mother for showing me the value in something made with love and care since ever I could remember. For showing me the magic world of sweets in Mexico, for giving me my first taste of raw milk, and for always encouraging us to find our own passions and fight for them despite what anyone thought (including her). To Jais and Sis, for always being my biggest motivation through my life and being with me always . . . even when we are far away. To my father, for always being brutally honest, for caring so much, for challenging me, and for being so loving every step of the way. To Manolo, for all your enthusiasm, love, support, and immense guidance in Mexico; I literally couldn't have done it without you! To my nieces Natushka and Luna Limón, for making me an aunt (the best feeling ever!) and continuously reminding me of how much love one can have.

To my grandmother, Ana, for your words and for caring so much. To my aunts, uncles, and cousins, whom I adore, but particularly to Michelle, Raque, and Cucus, for your constant presence, enthusiasm, and affection.

To my Danny, for being my rock and for standing with me through the days that I couldn't even stand myself. For your sweetness, love, kindness, and *apapachos* that surround me daily. For the bright colors you bring to my life and making me feel like the luckiest woman ever!

To Alexandra Zohn, for lovingly reminding me of the beauty that is within and right in front. For inspiring and pushing me toward a path of self love and reminding me to make the time to breathe!

Gracias Buhito, my almost brother, for being there not just for, but with me. Gracias Josefina for being an inspiration, for your generosity in time and heart, and for always making me feel the distance is not relevant.

To Brenda, for your wise words and for always believing.

To Mira, for helping me in the recipe testing but also for the heart and soul that you put into everything you do and everyone that surrounds you!

To Liza, Lesley, Shaw, Ron, and Leetal, for sharing the love of craftsmanship and good food that have nurtured and made me so happy.

To Gus, my *Tehueguejino*, for all the laughs and hugs and for your help in eating lots of ice cream!

To "Las Newyorkinas"—Chulis, Lyncita, Joab, Natalia, Gabi's, las Moni's.

Kareem, Julian, Marqui, Anna, Erin, Agatha, Daniela . . . for the moments that give me so much courage, love, and strength and for all the fun that allows me to breathe and reminds me to take a moment to enjoy. Your friendship and continuous love mean the world to me!

To Alex, my silent mentor and "sister," thank you for always inspiring me to push with heart and purpose and for sharing a passion that goes way beyond taste.

To Andrea, for taking care of so much and allowing me the space to dedicate to this book and for your friendship and continuous support.

To Nick and Maiana, for sharing some of the most delicious and lovely memories of ice cream making together; Andreuchis, for sharing the dream from the very beginning and for always being brutally honest.

To Karo, for your passion and commitment to La Newyorkina and the craft, and for being part of this book, and to Lily for all the hard work and enthusiasm.

To Sergi, for sharing the passion with me and for the dreams that have accompanied us through so much.

To Maya and Vicky, for your continuous support and for allowing me the time to dedicate to this book.

To Thierry for this, but also for sharing the love and passion for the craft and reminding me of the importance to shut out all the noise that can get in the way of passion and creativity.

To Angie and Alexis, for sharing a dream and for sharing this dedication with me . . . for reminding me daily to pay attention to the little things that make life beautiful!

Last but not least, to my dear friend Ian, to whom I've dedicated this book and miss so much! You continue to give me love and inspiration wherever you are. Thank you for always believing and being close. You are a big reason why this book exists, and I am so incredibly fortunate for our friendship. *Te extraño y quiero.*

ABOUT THE AUTHOR

As the country's most authoritative voice on Mexican sweets, FANY GERSON, has been featured in the *New York Times*, *Gourmet*, *Fine Cooking*, *Saveur*, *Food & Wine* and *New York* magazines, among others. She launched the acclaimed La Newyorkina, an artisanal Mexican frozen treats and sweets business, in 2010. She is also the chef and co-owner of Dough, a gourmet doughnut shop in New York. A graduate of the Culinary Institute of America, Fany has worked in a range of fine-dining kitchens around the world, including three-Michelin-starred Akelare in Spain and Eleven Madison Park in New York. She has written two books, *My Sweet Mexico*, which was nominated for a 2011 James Beard Award for Best Baking & Desserts cookbook, and *Paletas*. Fany also opened her first brick-and-mortar for La Newyorkina in October 2016 in the West Village of New York City.

MEASUREMENT CONVERSION CHARTS

VOLUME

U.S.	IMPERIAL	METRIC
1 tablespoon	½ fl oz	15 ml
2 tablespoons	1 fl oz	30 ml
¼ cup	2 fl oz	60 ml
⅓ cup	3 fl oz	90 ml
½ cup	4 fl oz	120 ml
⅔ cup	5 fl oz (¼ pint)	150 ml
¾ cup	6 fl oz	180 ml
1 cup	8 fl oz (⅓ pint)	240 ml
1¼ cups	10 fl oz (½ pint)	300 ml
2 cups	16 fl oz (⅔ pint)	480 ml
2½ cups	20 fl oz (1 pint)	600 ml
1 quart	32 fl oz (1⅔ pints)	1 l

TEMPERATURE

FAHRENHEIT	CELSIUS/GAS MARK
250ºF	120ºC/gas mark ½
275ºF	135ºC/gas mark 1
300ºF	150ºC/gas mark 2
325ºF	160ºC/gas mark 3
350ºF	175 or 180ºC/gas mark 4
375ºF	190ºC/gas mark 5
400ºF	200ºC/gas mark 6
425ºF	220ºC/gas mark 7
450ºF	230ºC/gas mark 8
475ºF	245ºC/gas mark 9
500ºF	260ºC

LENGTH

U.S.	METRIC
¼ inch	6 mm
½ inch	1.25 cm
¾ inch	2 cm
1 inch	2.5 cm
6 inches (½ foot)	15 cm
12 inches (1 foot)	30 cm

WEIGHT

U.S./IMPERIAL	METRIC
½ oz	15 g
1 oz	30 g
2 oz	60 g
¼ lb	115 g
⅓ lb	150 g
½ lb	225 g
¾ lb	350 g
1 lb	450 g

INDEX

Library of Congress Cataloging-in-Publication Data
Names: Gerson, Fany, author.
Title: Mexican ice cream : beloved recipes and stories / Fany Gerson; photography by
    Justin Walker and Fernando Gomez Carbajal.
Description: First edition. | California : Ten Speed Press, [2017] | Includes
    bibliographical references and index.
Identifiers: LCCN 2016051341 (print) | LCCN 2016054146 (ebook)
Subjects: LCSH: Ice cream, ices, etc. | Frozen desserts. | Desserts—Mexico.
    | Cooking, Mexican. | LCGFT: Cookbooks.
Classification: LCC TX795 .G468 2017 (print) | LCC TX795 (ebook) | DDC
    641.86/2—dc23
LC record available at https://lccn.loc.gov/2016051341

Hardcover ISBN: 978-1-60774-777-2
eBook ISBN: 978-1-60774-778-9

Printed in China

Design by Betsy Stromberg

10 9 8 7 6 5 4 3 2 1

First Edition